The Teacher's Survival Guide SECOND EDITION

JENNY GRAY

Consultant:
James R. Erickson, Principal
Norte del Rio High School
Sacramento, California

Drawings by Robert Haydock

FEARON PUBLISHERS, INC.
Belmont, California

Library of Congress Catalog Card Number: 73-83493.

ISBN-0-8224-6795-X.

Printed in the United States of America.

Contents

Preface

When the first edition of this book came out, I received a number of indignant letters. The writers challenged what they took to be the "authoritarian" attitudes expressed in the book. "Why must the teacher play this adversary role?" they asked. "Why can't he relax and enjoy his students?"

Each question carries its own curious assumption. The first implies that the role of leader and guide amounts to the same thing as the role of enemy, which on the face of it strains common sense. The second implies that if the teacher is a successful leader and guide, he automatically forfeits enjoyment.

Not only is this last assumption false, its exact reverse is more likely to be true. Our enjoyment of any activity is enhanced when we know we're good at it. The teacher who masters the skills necessary for his profession, including handling his discipline problems, will be far more likely to relax and enjoy his students than the one who doesn't!

In preparing this second edition, I was startled to realize how much society has changed in the last few years. Some of the present-day social problems were so rare when the first edition was published that they didn't deserve mention. The word "drugs," for example, didn't appear at all. Yet by the time the book had been on the market a year, drug abuse by students had become a major concern of educators in our larger cities and was already spreading to smaller cities and towns. Knowing how to handle a freaked-out student became a top-priority bit of classroom expertise.

Or take unwed mothers, another radical change. Certainly that situation has existed for generations, but it rarely surfaced. In recent years, however, court decisions have forced the issue into the open. Social mores have relaxed. Florence Crittenden Homes, once overcrowded havens of respectability, are everywhere closing for lack of customers. Today's unwed mothers are staying in school and keeping their babies—with no apologies asked and none offered.

Other problems such as theft and school fights, have intensified in the years since the first edition of this book was published. Suicide has become one of the leading causes of death among young people, forcing teachers and administrators to pay more attention to this threat than they once did. In many schools, the student-rights issue has developed into the stickiest wicket of all, threatening in a few cases to turn the overall educational effort into a theatre of the absurd.

But such observations only partially satisfy the demand of the moment. The function of a preface is to justify the book's existence. This book exists because far too many high school teachers enter their classrooms unprepared for the discipline problems that await them. They give up too quickly and leave the profession—a tragic waste. It is the purpose of this book to smooth a few rough spots, discipline-wise, and perhaps bridge a chasm or two.

Jenny Gray

The Teacher's Survival Guide

"A Disciplinarian? Me?"

"I was hired to teach, not to make kids behave." One often hears new teachers protest in this vein, and their objections are easy to understand. They may have spent two or three years learning methods, curriculum, and the subtleties of test construction. They thought that was what teaching was all about.

Well, it is and it isn't. Teaching a teen-ager in today's schools is like the farmer whopping his mule over the head with a two-by-four: First you have to get his attention.

Getting the attention of adolescents in today's secondary schools is a challenge, to say the least. Enough of a challenge to give the unprepared teacher a bad case of the vapors. State legislators make it worse by passing laws requiring all youth of the state, regardless of career goals, to attend school until age 16, 17, or even (in California) 18. The lawmakers want citizens of the state to be well educated, and there's nothing wrong with that.

But in practice, such laws incarcerate a resentful minority who are impatient to be about their life's business of earning a living. And the resentment spills over onto the Establishment figure nearest at hand, the teacher in the classroom.

Added to the compulsory-attendance problem is the swiftly changing nature of our society. Values shift so suddenly that one can't be surprised to find youngsters behaving as though there were no values at all. Change breeds insecurity which in turn breeds aggressiveness. At one time, "the way Daddy did it" was a reliable guide for young people, but no longer. When Daddy was in his teens, he didn't sit next to a dope pusher in English class. Daddy went to school with kids the same color he was— none of this integration stuff. There were bad boys when Daddy went to school, but even the worst of them never hid sawed-off shotguns in their lockers.

This isn't to say that teachers had no discipline problems in the golden days of yesteryear. There have always been discipline problems in public schools and always will be, kids being kids and sometimes having unorthodox ideas of what constitutes fun. Another reason for discipline problems is that public schools are just that—public. Everybody goes. The future heroes, prophets, and pillars of the community will be right there in your classes. So, alas, will be those at the other end of the public spectrum. And there will be even a larger percentage of the latter than will be found in the adult population. Still in their teens, the criminals and psychopaths of the future are too young yet to have gotten themselves locked up so they are no longer a threat to society. At this age, they're running around loose threatening society— and attending school. Some will be sitting in your class threatening *you.*

Classroom discipline is a big order for teachers in general and especially so for the novice in particular. Sad to say, there's no way to slice the problem down the middle with teaching on one side and discipline on the other. In the first place, the procedures that bring about good teaching are quite often the very ones that automatically bring about good classroom control and vice versa. And in the second place, whether or not it's spelled out at the time the new teacher signs a contract, he is most certainly hired to make kids behave *as well as* to teach. If he can't control the students in his classroom, he is of no use whatever to the school.

So it's not a question of either-or, but a matter of both or none. A pedagogical omelet, you might say, that resists unscrambling.

Control in the classroom is necessary for several reasons, all of them good. First of all, a school is a place for learning; a teacher, by definition, is committed to this goal. The teacher is there to teach the students. Where rowdiness and insolence hold sway, learning still takes place, certainly; but the results aren't likely to be compatible with the curriculum goals of the school, no matter how permissive the school's philosophy may be.

Secondly, from the moment he signs a contract, the teacher shares with the public school a tacit obligation to society. In the main, we allow ourselves to be governed by duly elected persons and their representatives. This is the only way our society can function in an orderly way. It is not good, therefore, if our young people become adept at the fine art of insurrection. The teacher who allows students to victimize him in his classroom indirectly encourages them to victimize the man at the newsstand, the stranger in the park, and the cop on his beat.

True, there are emotionally unstable students who, for therapeutic reasons, need to express their hostilities in some way. In these cases, it is important for the teacher to enlist the aid of other professionals on the school staff so that a student's aggression may be rechanneled into wholesome outlets. Above all, the teacher should avoid encouraging further development along unwholesome lines.

The hostile student is a victim of his own anger. He cannot save himself—he cannot hope to make himself acceptable to society—without the help of the professional people around him. If they fail to show him good ways to substitute for his bad ways and help him to make the transition, where can he turn? Furthermore, the teacher has an obligation to the other students who are the actual or potential victims of the emotional cripple. The teacher must maintain control of his class both to restrain the one and to protect the other.

Their protestations to the contrary notwithstanding, the need of young people for control, guidance, and protection from their own folly is as real as their need for food and sleep. Teacher popularity polls beyond number indicate that students reserve their highest accolades for the teacher who, ignoring good-natured taunts and complaints, maintains the steady pressure required to get the best behavior and the best work from them. New teachers invariably react with surprise when they discover for the first time that the vast majority of young people prefer firmly controlled, well-planned classes. A picnic atmosphere is fun for a while, but it soon palls for all but the farthest-out young patrons.

This only proves, of course, that adolescents are people like the rest of us. Human beings hunger for and respond favorably to order. We all want to know what's going to happen and when. We want to know what the rules are and what will happen if they are disobeyed. Knowing where we stand gives us a nice feeling. Call it "security."

Good classroom discipline is necessary for maintaining good teacher relations, good public relations, and a proper school image. The noise from a rowdy class can hinder learning activities in adjacent rooms or, if the walls are thin, in an entire wing or even the whole school. Visitors notice the pandemonium. Eyebrows are raised and word passes through the community, from whence it ultimately returns to perch, like a bird of doom, in the office of the school administrator. The teacher who allows such disturbance to continue unchecked is not likely to endear himself to his colleagues, and even less to the principal in the direct line of fire from the school's patrons.

One of the best reasons for maintaining an orderly classroom is that the teacher has an obligation to himself. Yesterday's teacher shortage has become today's glut, and if the novice with the unruly pupils can't control his students, there's another job applicant waiting to try. The new teacher may indeed be asked to resign, in time, but it's more likely that he'll resign of his own volition; his physical and emotional health will begin to crack under the strain. Depending on the state of his nerves, it will take perhaps a week, perhaps a year, for his students to drive him out. Day after day, week after week, the pattern will be the same:

"Hey! Somebody broke the pencil sharpener."

"Bob did. I saw him. He took off the handle. Search him, Teacher."

"You're a *&¢%¢ liar! I did not!"

"Bob, stop swearing and give me the handle to that pencil sharpener!"

"I ain't got it. You all the time accusing me of stuff I ain't done."

"Who threw that book?"

"What book? I didn't see no book."

"I can't sharpen my pencil."

"How's anybody gonna do anything when we can't sharpen our pencils? Helluva class *this* is!"

"Did you take the handle off the pencil sharpener?"

"*No!* So help me God, I ain't got it! Go ahead, search me!"

"Will you *stop swearing!*"

"How'm I gonna sharpen my pencil?"

"Owwwww! Herb hit me! @#%%& you, ************!"
(POW!)

"Sit down! Cut that out!"

"He hit me! You gonna let him get by with that?"

"We *are not* going to have that kind of language in this room!"

"What language are you talkin' about? What'd I say wrong?"

Tranquilizers may help, but they won't blot out the teacher's sickening realization that from some source he must summon the strength to overcome this situation by himself. Nobody can do it for him. It's the loneliest feeling in the world. Small wonder that some settle for the less exciting environment of a real estate office.

As school people euphemistically put it, students "put new teachers to the test." From the students' point of view, this "testing" makes a gruesome kind of sense. They want to find out how much this new teacher will tolerate, not only regarding actual physical misbehavior in the classroom, but about cheating, handing in homework assignments, "borrowing" books from the room, and all the rest of it. Once having found out that the new teacher won't tolerate misbehavior, the word gets around. The teacher may approach his second year with racing pulse, expecting a repeat performance of his first-year difficulties. But *if he held the line the first year,* he will discover to his astonishment that his second-year discipline problems never materialize at all. From then on, his teaching career may unfold as the rewarding vocation he expected it to be.

That first year is the ordeal by fire. Some don't make it. By virtue of temperament and background, a few teacher-candidates are doomed before they ever face a class.

Paradoxically, the teacher with a natural affection for young people and deep faith in their inherent goodness will be in for trouble. The first time a student turns in disgust from a reprimand muttering, "Aw, shove it," this teacher probably will be reluctant to fix the offender with an icy stare and curtly challenge him to repeat what he said. He is more likely to think that if he ignores such incidents they will go away. They won't. They will get worse.

Some individuals are too kind, too sympathetic, too peace loving ever to make very effective teachers. They can't say no and make it stick. No matter how plentiful the evidence may be to the contrary, they resist the realization that for the first weeks, or perhaps the first months, those creatures on the other side of his desk are The Enemy and must be dealt with accordingly.

Still others who will be in for trouble are those who have spent their own tender years in the sheltered confines of gentle, soft-spoken families. The unrestrained speech of today's teen-agers sets their teeth on edge. When exposed for the first time to the brutal candor of the young ("This room stinks. Can I open a window?"), they feel unduly offended and their reaction is out of all proportion to what is called for by the occasion. Confidences of the uninhibited shock them and they say so. The furtively scrawled grafitti on the blackboard revolts them and they say so.

Schoolteaching has its fang-and-claw aspects and it takes tough qualities to survive for long. The teacher candidate with tender cuticle should look elsewhere for a more compatible career.

An especially difficult time awaits the insecure beginner who wants his pupils to regard him as a pal. He fears the demands inherent in the supervisory role and rejects it as "too authoritarian." He refuses to provide the support needed by his young charges and tries instead to use them to fulfill his own needs. In no time at all, it will be the students who will be exploiting the teacher, not vice versa, and he'll wonder what went wrong.

A teacher candidate who is too timid to ask about classroom discipline is in for unpleasantness. He may not be sure which problems of student control he is responsible for and which should be handled by the vice principal, the nurse, or the counselor. Perhaps a student in his class spends the whole period, every day, crying. Another may insist he has a spastic colon; he asks to be excused to go to the restroom every day and is gone most of the period. Uncertain about what to do and reluctant to attract attention to his uncertainty, the teacher does not act, thus aggravating situations that should be dealt with as soon as they come up.

Such a situation is likely to develop with a person who has had little previous contact with young people who are similar to his student population. He can't distinguish between slightly abnormal behavior, which he is expected to handle himself, and extremely abnormal behavior, which should be referred to others on the school staff. This can happen not only to new teachers, but also to a teacher who moves from a senior to a junior high school, or from a "ghetto" school to a "country club" school. What is normal in one place may be abnormal in the other. All of these people must expect to undergo a period of adjustment.

Occasionally a teacher is foredoomed to have control problems because of what might be called "educational miscasting." A natural-born kindergarten teacher may prepare for teaching at the junior high school level, where she soon has discipline problems that are beyond her ability to handle. A scholarly, introspective teacher, who would be welcomed by the sons and daughters of

college professors in a university community, may find himself in the gut-level environment of an inner-city school where he comes across like a funny guy indeed. Hapless fifth graders may be taught close-order drill by a martinet who would be happier tangling with adolescents than diverting young children from their marbles and hopscotch.

The most common misplacements are not caused by teachers' unfortunate decisions, but by school-district expediency. A candidate who has prepared to teach history may be assigned a load of math or English classes because the district has more history teachers than it needs that year. So, in addition to his other orientation difficulties, the teacher must provide instruction in a subject he feels unsure of—or perhaps actively dislikes. His lack of preparation is soon evident to the students and it becomes a source of control trouble.

All these people have been miscast. They are teaching in the wrong places—wrong for them and wrong for their students. The bitter outcome of such a situation is that, as the years pass, successive classes of students become more hostile toward the teacher and he toward them. Perhaps the teacher has family obligations and is unable to make the necessary financial sacrifice to begin again somewhere else. He finds himself trapped in the job he has and the whole sorry business spirals to disaster.

The plight of the history teacher with the math classes may be buried for years, especially in a large school, unless the teacher takes it upon himself to press his case for a new assignment with the principal. To get the grease, the wheel needn't necessarily squeak loudly enough to be menacing—just persistently enough to be slightly annoying. But in most cases, squeak he must if he is going to get the assignment he wants.

Anyone entering the teaching profession should think seriously about where he can contribute his best teaching efforts. Maybe he will find students more attractive singly or at a distance than face to face in a group. If so, there are other alternatives. The field of education is no longer the narrow vocation it once was. A half-century ago, one was a classroom teacher or a principal, or perhaps both if the school were small. Over the years, schools have added the services of business managers, librarians, psychometricians, speech therapists, attendance officers, television personnel, and film technicians, to name a few. It takes all kinds to make the world of education go round, these days.

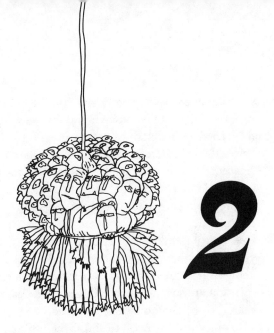

An Ounce of Prevention

"No one can tell you how to control your classes; this is something you will have to find out for yourself." Sound familiar?

Don't believe a word of it. You learn to control a class the same way you learn to weave, serve a buffet dinner, or ride the New York City subways. You read the directions, study the diagram, and talk to people who have done it. Then you do it yourself.

First of all, you need to have your goal clearly in mind. A behavioral objective, if you will. Your behavioral objective is that your students shall obey you. That's what this book is about. Whether we adults like it or not, discovering imaginative new ways to challenge authority is the great parlor game of American youth. As a teacher, you must checkmate all such attempts so that your students, discouraged by repeated failure, give up on you and shift their attention to other targets.

You don't especially want students to obey you with fear, because then they won't tell you important things like "The superintendent is coming down the hall to visit your room." It's better if they obey you in much the same spirit they would obey the captain of a team—because you're a good Joe and you're better than they are at whatever it is you're doing. This is called "respect." Although it might rankle to be forced to keep earning it week in and week out, that's the price you pay for tenure.

The acid test, which you must expect to fail the first semester and maybe even the first year, is what happens when you're absent from the room. The students may behave well when you're with them, but what do they do when you're called to the phone? Or what do they do with a substitute?

If you are successful at building good discipline habits in your students, you should be able to depend on them to regulate themselves in your absence—to finish the assignment or to leave the room in good order when they go. The ultimately successful teacher, like the ultimately successful parent, makes the child independent of him. The teacher strives to develop in the student those qualities of self-discipline that will one day enable him to teach himself.

You want to see an increase in good sportsmanship. There should be more consideration for the other fellow (including you!), a greater willingness to share and take turns. There should be a greater tendency in the group to be friendly and extend support, not to a few, but to all its members, to visitors, and to newly enrolled students. There should be a "we-ship" in your classes, born of the security that roots and flourishes when students realize that no individual will be threatened unless he himself originates the threat.

When it comes to noise, the decible count is only one measure of good control. You want your classes to be quiet, yes; but a quiet class doesn't necessarily mean there is good control. The students may all be asleep. Ask yourself the same question your supervisor will ask when he enters your room to observe: Is learning taking place here? Are the students quiet because they are absorbed in their schoolwork, or are they merely cowed?

There are noisy classes and noisy classes. Teen-agers cover up lack of confidence with loud talk and movement. When the members of the class are achieving and *know* of their achievement, this kind of noise will abate over a period of time. A successful—a truly successful—skit, debate, or discussion will generate an uproar of sorts. But this is "good" noise. This is learning noise, one of the nicest sounds in the world to hear. When all the students in the room are sitting on the edges of their seats and waving their hands frantically for permission to recite, you are doing a fine job of teaching.

There is the comfortable buzzing sound when small groups in the room are working together or students have paired off to study. There is that throbbing, electric silence when every student is so absorbed in what he is reading that he has completely lost touch with you, the school, the noises outside in the street— everything. Across the room a student finishes. He looks up dazed, closes his book, and stretches. You go to his desk, finger on your lips, to remind him not to disturb the others.

"Boy, that was a good story!" he whispers.

Marvelous, marvelous.

The best learning is something the student experiences as a total human being. It must engulf him so completely that he forgets himself, forgets disappointments, anxieties, and resentments. The noise in a classroom lets you know if this is happening. For a teacher, these learning noises are the payoff. Once you earn your

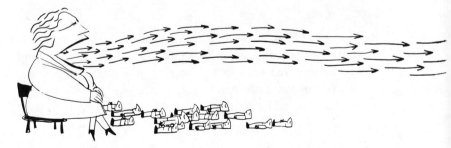

place as captain of the team, you have the power to produce the learning noise you desire in your classroom.

YOUR LOOKS

Funny, isn't it, how success in achieving any goal always seems to depend on the little things? Good classroom control depends on little things, sometimes even superficial things—like the way you look.

Though the new teachers seem to get better looking each year, nobody pretends that our profession has a monopoly on comeliness. In fact, particularly in young teachers, beauty of the face and form can be a handicap when the student population is age twelve or over. Discipline problems for women teachers tend to increase in direct ratio to how young and pretty they look. The same factor works against the good-looking young male teacher who can't understand why girls in his classes are so recalcitrant. Roiling glands make for noisy kids.

But grooming is another matter. Anybody can be well groomed. And anyone working with teen-agers had jolly well better be! Adolescents outdo every other segment of the population in finding fault. The faults of others—including teachers—forms a dreary staple of teen-age conversation. If you don't believe it, eavesdrop. You'll learn a lot. Bad breath, body odors, untidy hair, dirty hands, and soiled clothing are less easily forgiven than a poor grasp of the subject matter—and they make classroom control much more difficult.

YOUR VOICE

To control a class, you must be heard at the back of the room. You must be heard *clearly* at the back of the room. If you command the required volume and possess, in addition, such vocal flexibility that you can direct briskly or encourage gently enough to melt stones, you are lucky beyond anyone's right to expect.

If you do not possess such a voice, it is well worth several dollars' tuition and several semesters' work in some speech department to develop one. While you are there, you might make sure you aren't burdened with other speech handicaps, such as lisping, stuttering, or whistling sibilants. Be sure you aren't saying "he don't" for "he doesn't." And if you're from south of the Mason-Dixon Line, make sure you aren't saying "that's rat" instead of "that's right."

YOUR PREPARATION

Wasted time while the teacher hunts this, goes to get that, gives the wrong directions and then must correct them, or fiddles with the audio-visual equipment are marks of the amateur and should be avoided. Everyone respects a professional job and high school students are no exception. When students are busily engrossed in organized, well-planned schoolwork that has meaning for them, they simply do not misbehave. If the teaching is good, the control will probably be good, too. Each supports the other.

YOUR CLASSROOM

How curious that elementary teachers should be light-years ahead of us secondary teachers when it comes to tastefully decorated classrooms! Many of our breed seem to scorn beautiful surroundings as *lèse majesté*—a shortsighted attitude in the light of consumer research. If you want to sell something, pretty it up. If you want your students to buy your course of study, make your classroom attractive. Pots of plastic philodendron, for instance, require neither water nor a sunny spot, and they go far toward brightening up the place. Colorful pictures taped to construction paper relieve drabness. Bulletin boards can be superb visual aids for teaching a unit, setting a mood, or getting a point across. Over the years, most teachers build excellent files of display materials and ideas. The novice, short of time to prepare such materials and lacking the money to buy them ready made, may do well to recruit student committees for this work.

YOUR PHYSICAL LIMITATIONS

Take some thought for your nerves. When pressures build, your patience evaporates and discipline problems rush in to fill the vacuum. The best way to avoid pressure on your first assignment is to drop by school at least a week early to get your textbooks, teacher's manuals, curriculum guides, lesson plan book, and whatever, so you can get your homework out of the way ahead of time. (The principal will be there. Drop in to say hello. If he's in a mood to talk, listen.)

There will be interludes in your teaching career when you will stay one day ahead of the students; but this kind of high-wire stunt requires considerable skill and *sang-froid*, both of which you will develop later but don't have now. Once school starts, you will be so busy with records, memos, directives, and bulletins that the wiring in your head will approach the overload point. Do yourself a favor and study your textbooks early.

When you outline your lesson plans for the first few weeks, pay attention to the energy factor. Some lesson plans take a lot out of you; others don't. Don't, for example, schedule a lesson

plan that calls for showing two short films (to be projected by you) plus a chalkboard-illustrated lecture (given by you), the whole thing to be repeated for five or six successive classes. By 1 P.M. you won't care if school keeps or not, and by 4 P.M., forget it. This is assuming you have only one preparation. If you have two or more, it's even more important to avoid squandering your physical resources, because there'll be even greater demands on your mental ones.

Practice. It isn't enough to load, run, and rewind the tape, film, or filmstrip once. Go over this operation often enough so that you can talk and give your attention to the students while you're doing it.

Your lesson plans are more likely to be too short than too long. For every class, always have something extra to do in case the students finish early. When caught with your lesson plans down —and you will be (the film won't arrive, or the ditto machine will break down so that you can't run off the test you planned to give) —allow the students the extra time for study. *Do not* turn them loose for a "free time" session that, for the new teacher especially, is likely to get out of hand.

YOUR ASSIGNMENTS

Learn to write out instructions for homework assignments so that they are clear and easy for even your slowest students to understand. Then set aside a conspicuous place in your classroom, perhaps a section of the chalkboard, where homework assignments will always be written for easy student reference. Deadlines for projects, reports, and the like, should also be written there. Never let a student drag out the old "but I didn't know what I was supposed to do" chestnut. Keep your assignment board up to date, then the student must either produce the assignment or admit his own, not your, negligence.

Decide what formula you are going to follow in computing your grades. Will tests count for half of the semester grade or a third? Will reports or themes be required? If so, when? How will they average in on the semester grade? What arrangements will you have for the student to make up work he misses when he is absent? Be sure your students know these things.

YOUR FROWN

Spend some time practicing a menacing glare in front of your bathroom mirror. Pack all the disapproval you can muster into a baleful, wide-eyed stare. (A flicking jaw muscle adds a certain dash.) To govern by eye control is a talent of the master teacher. It saves voice and feet. Learn how to do it.

KNOW WHO'S COMING

You will have class rosters before classes begin. Take the time to study them. Getting to know your students as quickly as possible is an essential for good control. It will take you two or three days, perhaps a week, to get your seating charts in order.

When the students first come into your classroom, you can expect the compulsive talkers to arrange themselves so as to get the most conversational mileage out of the least distance. You will have to reseat them. The potential dropouts, in an effort to get as far away from school as the law allows, will choose the back seats. They are the ones you will want to seat closest to your desk, for they will need the most help—not recrimination, help.

FIRST IMPRESSIONS

At the beginning of every period, you will call your class to order. The first day or two you won't need to. The students will be on their good behavior, both for your benefit and for the benefit of many of their fellow students, who will also be new to them. They will be quiet because they are curious. As the newness wears off, the chatter level will rise. When the room is noisy, wait. Don't begin until the students have noticed you standing before them and have stopped talking. You may need to help matters along. "May I have your attention, please?" "May I have *your* attention, too, Joe?" "I'm waiting for you, Evelyn." Don't shout. If you do, you'll lose.

Do something that first day to show your subject matter proficiency. Read a selection from a play, make a tool, draw a picture, or kick a ball. Tell your students something about yourself. Married? Children? Where did you go to college? Former experiences in jobs, teaching, armed forces? Win trophies in wrestling? Karate? Knife throwing? Little things like that.

From the first day, refuse to let students get up and walk out on you in mid-sentence when the bell rings to signal the end of the period. The bell doesn't dismiss the class, the teacher does.

DON'T . . .

Don't let students call you by your first name. Kids this pushy will need to have the message clearly spelled out for them in short, easy words: "Don't call me Pete. I am your teacher. Call me Mr. Smith."

Don't tolerate naps. "Sleep on your own time, not mine. Sorry."

Don't tolerate throwing in the classroom. This will start innocently enough with a student tossing a pencil to his buddy in the next row, or a wad of paper into the wastepaper basket six feet away. "Go get the paper. Return to your seat. Get up. Carry it to the wastebasket. Drop it in. Return to your seat. Don't throw *anything, any time,* in this room."

Don't tolerate filthy language. "The place for locker room talk is in the locker room, not here." Glare when you say it.

Don't tolerate even playful scuffling. "Any more horsing around like that and you're in serious trouble. Sit down and keep your hands and feet to yourself." *Really* glare when you say this.

YOUR DESK

From the beginning, refuse to let students get in the habit of making themselves at home around your desk. Don't let them sit in your chair when you're not in it or hang over you when you are. Girls, especially, will give men teachers the business about this. If not outmaneuvered, they will lean in provocative ways. The male teacher may find it necessary to pull out a drawer to force a girl student to stand back, put a stack of books on the edge of the desk where she's leaning, or best of all, stand up.

A woman teacher will have her handbag in her desk, which is an additional reason for keeping students at a distance. If she's smart, she'll take other precautions against theft, such as leaving valuable jewelry and large sums of money at home where they'll be safe.

A good teacher won't spend much time at a desk, anyway. Train your students to raise their hands when they need help. When they do, go to them. Stay on your feet, among your students where you're needed.

HOW FRIENDLY?

In the classroom, find a happy medium between friendliness and aloofness. If you have spent a great deal of time with young people before, you won't need to look for this happy medium at all; you will automatically assume the attitude that's right for you.

Then, too, especially if you're with classes you know ahead of time will be tough, you'll move that attitude a bit to the "aloof" side of the scale during the first few days of school. The tougher the school, the farther to that side of the scale you'll move.

Seasoned teachers always "start out hard." They don't smile much. They don't crack jokes. Why? A teacher can't find out how a class is going to shape up until he's been with the group for a week or two. With some classes, you find within a few days that you can relax a little, perhaps a lot. But with other classes, you must exercise vigilance every minute the students are in the room; you may not be able to smile at them until you tell them goodbye in June. It isn't always individual students that make the difference, either. Sometimes it's the "mix" that's particularly volatile.

COACH, DON'T CRITICIZE

The way you take hold during the first few days of school will determine how your students size you up and react to you; so will your attitude toward them. If you must give a student an F on a paper, explain why or write a few words of encouragement to soften the blow. A student's report may come back to him with "Not very original" scrawled across the top. This is criticism— negative, cold, and not particularly effective. The teacher may have written instead, "Your written work will be more interesting if you try for more variety in your sentences. See me after class and I'll show you what I mean." This is coaching, which gets better results. Does this kind of thing make a difference in class-room control? Try it and see.

HOW TO HANDLE TROUBLEMAKERS

A teacher loses face by yelling. You don't need to yell, anyway. There's a non-yell formula you can use in dealing with misbehavior in the classroom. It goes like this:

1. A student is shooting rubber bands at his girlfriend across the aisle. Look at him but continue to direct the classroom discussion as though nothing were wrong. Do not pause. Never allow a discipline problem to interrupt your work if you can possibly help it.
2. Usually, you will be able to catch the erring student's eye. Deliver the baleful glare you practiced in front of the mirror. If the student continues his disruptive behavior, point your finger at him and shake your head to indicate clearly to him that he is to stop. Continue the discussion without a pause.
3. If the student is so engrossed in his misbehavior that he doesn't realize you have seen him, continue the lesson and walk slowly toward his seat. As your voice grows louder, he will become conscious of your approach and glance in your direction.
4. By this time, he has gotten the message, all right. If he persists, you are dealing with a student who is deliberately challenging you. Do not lose your temper. Do not for one moment lose your train of thought. Keep on with the class-room work but continue to move toward him.
5. If he stops before you arrive at his seat, continue on your way to him, anyway. Stand beside him and conduct your class from there for a minute or so. Let him sweat. When the other students' attention is elsewhere, lean over the offending student and, in a whisper or voice so low that no

one else can hear, tell him emphatically that when you correct him you expect him to obey immediately. Do not argue.

6. If you know he has seen you but he persists in his misbehavior even after you have arrived at his seat, you have a serious problem. He has gone beyond challenging your authority; he is openly displaying his contempt for you. Spare him no mercy. Lean over him and whisper or speak very quietly in his ear. No one but the culprit should hear what you say.

Deliver the nastiest, most abusive attack on his character, his personality, and his appearance that you are capable of. Do not threaten. You don't need to—you are in charge of your classroom and you intend to stay in charge. Do not use profanity. Do not malign members of his family or allude to his race, creed, or ethnic background. *Do not touch him.* Nothing should register on your face but a pleasant, rather noncommital expression. The weapon is what you are saying to him. Any entertainment that is provided for the class is in the squirming of the culprit himself. Ignore any attempt at rebuttal on his part. Continue to insult him with the pleasant expression on your face. He knows instinctively that if he loses his temper, his strategy backfires. It was you he intended to make a laughingstock, not himself. Only later will he realize that he dare not repeat to his friends what you said to him. After all, some of the things you said might be things his friends already think but have not said to his face. When he has subsided, tell him you don't want any more trouble out of him.

7. Then, forget it. Continue with your class as though nothing had happened. In your future dealings with that student, act as though nothing has happened. (He'll want to avoid you, but don't let him.) Of the seven points, this last one is the most important for good long-term classroom control. You will have differences with many students over the school year. To mull over their transgressions like old photographs in an album is to deny them the freedom to redeem themselves and grow into better people. Take care of the offense *when it happens.* Take care of it *thoroughly.* Then forget it.

Sometimes you will be outraged to discover that although you are willing to forget a classroom peccadillo, the student isn't. Although you caught him in the act of tearing the page out of the classroom dictionary and he richly deserved the stiff reprimand you gave him, he may withdraw into a black sulk for several days. He is punishing *you* for punishing *him!* The best thing to do is ignore it. It will require the patience of Job to keep from popping this kid a good one on the mouth, but don't. Someday his wife will. He can't sue *her.*

One cautionary note before we leave the classroom set-to. You won't always catch the culprit red-handed. Unless you are such a marvel that you can referee twelve ping-pong games at once, eight of which are being played behind a four-foot hedge, a time will inevitably come when you collar a student for something he really didn't do. It isn't because of his denial that you will know this. All but the most docile will deny that they threw the eraser across the room or dotted the ceiling with spitballs. What may arouse your suspicion that you tapped the wrong offender will be the intense degree of his surprise and indignation. He will stammer and redden; veins will stand out on his neck.

Let matters stand for the moment. As the class is leaving, invent a pretext to question a student who was sitting next to or behind the accused and see what you can find out privately. If you were wrong, quietly go to his seat the next day and apologize. He'll spread the word, never fear. You will gain far more by admitting you were wrong than you would by clinging to your error.

CONFISCATED GOODS

From time to time you will have to confiscate things. Although most students, when asked, will wait until after class to show their friends the bauble made in shop class or the snake's skull picked up on the way to school, there will be some who either can't or won't wait and the resulting hubbub creates a disturbance. In that case, you must sometimes ask that the attention-getter be given to you for safekeeping until class is over. Never keep such an item. It is not yours. It is a prized possession and should be returned to the owner at the end of the period.

CORPORAL PUNISHMENT

In the teacher's handbook that you'll receive when you start to work, there will be a section on corporal punishment. The teacher should know the state laws and the district policy regarding corporal punishment and know them well. Regardless of whether state law expressly forbids it, a new teacher is well advised *never* to touch a student in anger. *Never.* This means shoving, shaking, pinching, jerking at clothing, stepping on toes, and every other kind of physical contact. In cases of incorrigible students (and there are such things; the man who said there were no bad boys was seeing through a glass eye darkly), the school has recourse to suspension or expulsion. Later, when you have time, you will want to familiarize yourself with these laws, too.

"THE OFFICE"

There may or may not be instructions in the teacher's handbook about sending students to the vice principal's office. It's funny how nobody ever comes right out and tells a new teacher just how this arrangement works. Your principal wants you to feel the security of knowing that the administration will back you up when discipline problems arise. Yet if every teacher sent students to "the office" for every minor infraction, a larger staff would be required in the office than in the classrooms! So the matter is glossed over in the expectation that if the new teacher runs into something he can't handle, he'll send the student down. And this is exactly what you should do—with no apologies, no defensive explanations—so long as you send the student *as a last resort.*

There are degrees of correcting a misbehaving student. The rank order goes something like this:

First offense: "Joe, please be quiet."

Second offense: "Joe, did you hear me? I asked you to be quiet."

Third offense: (privately) "When I tell you to be quiet, that's just what I want you do do. Open your book and get to work."

Fourth offense: (also privately) "Listen to me, you pimply little bag of greasy hot air, etc., etc."

Fifth offense: (outside in the hall) "I told you four times to stop talking and you're still talking. So what's with you?

Sixth offense: "Go to the office."

You will find that a crisis with a student seldom "just happens." Generally, it will build over a period of several days. Thus, you are able to forewarn the vice principal about the student before you find it necessary to send him down, which for any teacher is by far the best policy. Having already heard your version of the trouble, the vice principal won't find himself forced to rely on the student's version.

"The office" is like a savings account. Draw on it all the time and there's not much protection. If you sent five students a day to the office, they'll get a slap on the wrist and that's about all. If you send one a month, he might see the business end of a paddle if the law allows. If you send only one student a *year,* you might just as well tell the kid good-bye. The vice principal might think the offense warrants expulsion!

THE TEACHER'S HANDBOOK

The teacher's handbook will give school policy about absences, tardiness, and class deportment in general. Read these rules carefully. Posting a typed or printed summary of them on the bulletin board is helpful.

Some schools turn the rule-making responsibility over to a student council, which is a good idea. The rules may be printed in a student handbook and a copy given to every young person enrolled in the school. Twenty minutes of class time the first day may be devoted to a discussion of these rules—an excellent practice. Many students will know the rules quite well already. What none of them will know is whether *you* know them and, if you do, how strictly you intend to enforce them.

There is always student pressure to interpret these rules liberally and administrative pressure to interpret them strictly. The teacher's judgment must be mature enough to judge each case on its own merits. The *new* teacher, however, short on experience and long on the desire to make good, is best advised to stick as closely to the book as possible. When in doubt, ask.

STUDENTS' RIGHTS I: THE DRESS CODE

There will be rules written down somewhere about the student dress code. How long may long hair be? How short may short pants be? How bare may various portions of the student's anatomy be? In the recent past, school districts have lost court suits over the matter, and the new teacher is brash indeed who takes it upon himself to force a dress code issue before checking to see if he has the support of his superiors.

In many schools, the new teachers on the staff will be given careful instructions as part of the orientation procedure. If you are given no definite policy guidelines, study the printed code carefully, then go slow. If a student appears in your class the first week of school who might be arrested on the street for indecent exposure, ease the student out before class begins. Simply say, "I believe you are in violation of the dress code. We teachers have been instructed to send violators to the vice principal."

(Must it be said? Yes, perhaps it must. Teachers themselves should adopt a mode of dress that is well within the boundaries set by requirements for students.)

STUDENTS' RIGHTS II: DISCRIMINATION

Be he Japanese, Chinese, Chicano, black, Jewish, WASP, or etc., the teacher with a strong personal prejudice against another religious or ethnic group will find himself in danger of losing his job if he tries to teach students belonging to that group. The more intense the prejudice, the more difficult it will be for him to hide it. He will find it almost impossible to deal with all his students on equal terms. His wisest course is to transfer out of the situation.

Minority groups are especially sensitive to hassling by the teacher that seems to jeopardize what they feel to be their rights. On most discipline questions, the teacher can rely on support from the principal, but on this particular issue—racial discrimination—the principal is especially vulnerable. A hot-headed teacher can embroil his principal in weeks of grilling by NAACP and civil rights officials and lawyers. If the principal refuses to run interference for the teacher but lets him take his own lumps, the teacher shouldn't be especially surprised.

Sometimes teacher hassling is more imagined than real, and at such times it is an easy matter to set matters straight. If black or Chicano students want to prepare research reports on subjects of racial interest, arrange for them to get what they want. If the Jewish students plan to be absent for religious holidays, arrange your lesson plans so there will be as little work as possible to make up when they return.

Be scrupulously fair about grading, about rewards and penalities, about marking tardies and absences. Keep careful records. At a school board inquiry, those records might turn out to be the best friend you ever had. (See *Your Records*, p. 31.)

STUDENTS' RIGHTS III: SUSPENSIONS, EXPULSIONS

Not many years ago, the teacher was seldom involved in the more serious school punishments. Today the teacher's evidence may be required in a quasi-judicial hearing with lawyers and parents at the time a student is suspended or expelled. The school is protecting itself against future lawsuits. Don't over- or under-testify. Keep it straight. Keep it cool.

TEACHERS' RIGHTS

Occasionally one hears of a (mercifully) rare school district where the students' rights issue has been carried to incredible extremes. A small group of students, seldom more than 1 percent of the total enrollment, will insist on their "right" to hire and fire the faculty, dictate the curriculum, shout unprintable abuse at teachers and administrators, instigate gang wars in the cafeteria, come to class any time they choose, and otherwise make as flamboyant nuisances of themselves as their imaginations will allow. Within the last few years, such pressures on teachers and administrators have taken their toll in fatal heart attacks, strokes, asthma attacks, and suicides.

Is there no such thing as rights for teachers and administrators? Why is the American Civil Liberties Union interested in a youth's right to attend public school, no matter what, but is uninterested in a teacher's right to pursue a vocation free of gratuitous malice, harrassment, and threat of bodily harm? Does the school board owe its personnel a minimal guarantee of safety while discharging professional duties? If so, how far must a discipline situation in a school deteriorate before the school board moves to deliver on its guarantee? Perhaps it's time for teachers and administrators in such districts to exert pressure of their own on community patrons and irresponsible school boards. If militant minorities

charge injustice and walk out to force the injustice to be corrected, then surely school personnel can play at the same game!

SECURITY

Many schools have strict policies about leaving money in teachers' desks. Proceeds from the candy sale, club dues, and so on, should be turned in promptly. Instance after instance can be cited where a school was broken into during the night (repair windows and door locks, $25) and a locked dest hacked to bits (replace desk, $300). Net gain to the thief: $2.50 in the PTA membership dues envelope.

Every school has its own standard procedures for securing the classroom before leaving at night. This information will be in the teacher's handbook. In some districts the custodians lock the windows and doors; in others the teachers customarily do this. In schools with untrustworthy neighbors and low budgets, all audiovisual equipment must be locked up at night; in others it may remain in place in the room, set up and ready for use from day to day.

Schools with a high break-in rate may prohibit teachers from locking desks, cabinets, and files. Classroom doors may be left unlocked and standing open at night. The same with vending machines—locks are more expensive to replace than the pencils and candy bars the thieves might steal. All money, audiovisual equipment, student records, and supplies are locked in a vault at night. Teachers are warned not to leave personal effects they consider valuable in their rooms.

It is idiotic for a teacher to carry more than a few dollars at school. Make change for students? If a youngster needs change for more than a five dollar bill, he should be sent to the office for it. A student with a bill larger than a five is suspect, anyway.

If the teacher intends to go shopping after school and has cashed a check for this purpose, he might put the money in an envelope and give it to the office personnel for safekeeping. A woman teacher should never leave her handbag where students will be tempted to rifle it. Carrying or wearing expensive jewelry is a silly risk. It's in poor taste, too.

YOUR RECORDS

The seeds of poor control are often sown in sloppy records. Did the student fail to turn in his written report on time because he was absent? He insists he was, but your gradebook doesn't show this absence. Are you keeping a girl from graduating because you gave her bad grades, or has she kept herself from graduating because she made the bad grades with no help from you at all? Your gradebook should reflect these things, and it should reflect them accurately and consistently.

It's always better policy to "compute" grades than to "give" them, by the way. If the student is convinced his grade depends on his effort to learn the subject matter, he will learn the subject matter. If his grade depends on learning how to butter up the teacher, he will learn to butter up the teacher.

Don't allow yourself to be intimidated by parents (or sometimes, surprisingly enough, other teachers) who insist that "Keith is a straight-A student" when your gradebook clearly shows Keith to be a C-minus student in your class. Don't argue. Just bring out your gradebook.

TEACHER'S PETS

Students respect a teacher who enforces rules equally for all students. You wouldn't be human if you didn't have favorites, of course. What you need to guard against is the temptation to favor them openly—"openly" to other students or "openly" to *them*.

The same will hold true when the teacher develops a crush on a whole class. What often happens is that the favored class or the favored student will get out of line (partly your fault; you will relax because you are enjoying them) and you will have some straighening-out to do. What with one thing and another, you can count on it that the class you find delightful the first week of school *won't* be the one you are finding delightful by the first of November. You will probably have a different favorite by Christmas and still another by Easter. But your favorites should remain your private business; nothing but harm will result if you let the students know.

BE CONSISTENT

It works against your interests as a teacher and compounds your control problems to interpret school rules strictly today and ignore them tomorrow, check the roll one way today and another way tomorrow, or use a different method every day for collecting students' papers. Decide at the beginning how you want to do these things, and stick to your procedure.

Personal relationships with students are subject to the same rules as personal relationships with your friends or members of your family. When you blow hot and cold, nobody knows what to expect and your presence generates a certain uneasiness. This is even more true of the students who are subject to your authority in the classroom.

Tact is necessary. The teacher must be frank in order to achieve his goal, but the truth need not go stark naked. "Put clothes on the truth" by telling a story, or by using such phrases as "Perhaps if ...," "Would you like to try ...," and "Had you ever thought that if you. ..."

DON'T BE BULLDOZED

Teen-agers get carried away with their enthusiasms. They will demand your permission to let them do such and such *now*, even though neither they nor you know anything about the business at hand. When you are hurried into a yes or no decision, always say no. Then take time to get the facts. It is easier to change the no to yes later than the hasty yes to a sadder-but-wiser no.

WHOSE FAULT?

"Mama made me the jerk I am today" is a favorite theme of the young, and no wonder. Freudian influence is waning in our culture, but variations on "It's all Mama's fault" still appear in every medium from comic books to musical comedy. In many cases, the teacher will have an opportunity to meet the student's mother and, having done so, will be inclinded to agree with the student that Mama did, indeed, pass on some of her less attractive qualities. But the teacher's reason for being in the classroom is to bring about change for the better, not to accept imperfection passively. If the teacher goes along with the sterile "Mama's-fault" philosophy, he will soon find himself with nothing to chew on but air.

Granting that imperfection is Mama's fault, what then? Mama is clearly imperfect, too. Who is to blame for her imperfection, Grandma? And is Great-grandma to blame for Grandma's imperfection? And Great-great-grandma to blame, and so on and on? The jerks of today's younger generation aren't unique phenomena of the twentieth century. There have been jerks ever since Cain.

Well, then, what are today's jerks going to do about it? Will they continue to visit the sins of jerkism on their own children and on their children's children, or do they intend to break the vicious chain and do something constructive to stop being a jerk? It is in their power to do so. It is in the teacher's power to make them *want* to do so.

HELLOOOOOOOOO DOWN THERE

The new teacher needs to know when to speak up and when to shut up. In a large school, a new teacher is likely to disappear like a rock in a bucket of mud. His difficulties may go unnoticed for months or even years. Don't let this happen to you. You're too young to die. Let people know you're there. Establish lines of communication with the counselors, the dean, and the vice principal. Drop by various offices from time to time to talk over discipline problems that bother you. The janitors, the secretaries, the nurse, and the cafeteria people can give you all kinds of useful information. Cultivate friendship with experienced teachers who can answer your questions.

Spend some time in the teacher's lounge or the faculty dining room *listening*. At this stage of your development, you have more to gain by listening to experienced teachers talk then by hovering over your desk in your room grading papers. Take the papers home and hover over them on your own time. Your first year in the classroom will be one of the most gruelling of your life anyway, so you may as well resign yourself to an eighteeen-hour day and relax.

Knowing when to shut up is as important as knowing when to speak up. For example, never discuss a student with or within earshot of another student. This kind of thing invariably finds its way back—tinctured with malice—to the one you least want to hear it. Don't go around bearing tales to students or anybody else about fellow staff members, their troubles or shortcomings. A fink by any other name (such as "unprofessional person") still smells bad.

KEEP YOUR PERSPECTIVE

We school people deal in book learning only, and there are many other kinds—some that go so far beyond us that we are left behind in a cloud of chalk dust. Remind yourself that Albert Einstein did not pass his entrance examinations to college, that Herbert Hoover repeated freshman English at Stanford and failed it the second time as well as the first, and that Dwight Eisenhower ranked next to the bottom of his West Point graduating class. You will be obliged to fail many students, because that's the way everybody plays the game. But when you must fail a student, you can refuse to let the mark become a personal rejection. He may have failed this particular task at this particular time, but it's rather brash to conclude that he has failed as a human being.

Most important of all, keep your perspective about yourself. Allow yourself ten full-dress blunders your first year. That should hit it about right. As you fall in and out of your successive pits of error, note that the earth has not been riven asunder and the skies have not turned blood red. Nothing like that happened when the country's other two million teachers made their first-year mistakes. No disaster is ever so dreadful that it can't be remedied by time and a sense of humor.

The best thing you can hope for your first year—and I fervently wish it for you—is that you have both students and colleagues with whom you can share a good laugh.

Getting Down to Cases

The teacher must wait years to see the harvest of his labors. Sometimes it isn't until the children of his former students come to him that he finds he may pride himself on his efforts of twenty years before. With great effort, he was able to teach the first generation to "talk English good." Thanks to that effort, the second generation may learn to "speak English well."

This is true in the area of curriculum. It is also true in the area of common ethics. The school must take the long view. There is the boy who is caught with a cache of stolen pencils. The parents are summoned to the school for a conference. Upon being told of the theft, the distraught mother, who works as a stenographer in a government office, upbraids her son for taking such a foolish risk. It wasn't necessary, she tells him. Only the week before, she had copped a dozen new pencils from her office to replenish the supply at home!

The mother has been stealing for fifteen years. No one has ever caught her or made her feel it was wrong in any way. She sees no reason why she shouldn't go on stealing property that doesn't belong to her for another fifteen years, and she probably will. For the boy, it is different. He steals from the school once, is caught, and will remember the embarrassment for a long time to come. Who knows? With a little luck, perhaps the third generation won't steal at all!

Keeping petty crime nipped in the bud is as much the obligation of the teacher as giving a subject-matter test. The difficulty with the new teacher is that, because of his innocence, he's apt to nip in all the wrong places. The person on the school staff most likely to show him the right places will be the administrator who heads the discipline department. His title may be vice principal, assistant principal, dean of boys, dean of girls, or head counselor. Often the discipline problems are shared between a dean of boys and a dean of girls.

These officials are full-time chastisers, chaser-downers, and (when all else fails) chucker-outers of evildoers. They maintain liaison with the police department, parole officers, the juvenile court, the FBI, welfare officials, detention home officials, and parents of young offenders—sometimes even with the parole officers of the parents! They are the officials who play the Stern Parent role for the school establishment. They do the dirty work. They seldom deal with the majority of decent kids who people our secondary schools, only with the small minority who are thugs, punks, and brats.

The daily pressures on the Stern Parents are fantastic. The dean of boys, because he is male, gets especially rough treatment. Indignant daddies and mommies will threaten to come to school and tear him apart if he lays a hand on Sonny. He frequently does and sometimes they do. There are other thrills shared by whoever happens to be carrying the load: The tires on their cars are more apt to be slashed than anyone else's. Their lives will be threatened fairly regularly. They will be likely to have unlisted telephones so they can get some peace at home. They may also have facial tics and stomach ulcers.

These officers won't be playing Stern Parent roles because they enjoy it. They'll be doing it because somebody must do it, and do it well, if the school isn't to fall into the hands of its lawless elements. Moreover, this assignment happens to be one of the rungs on the ladder that leads to the principal's job. Every principal has gone through it at one time or another. When he did well as Stern Parent, he (or she) was promoted to Benign Parent, or principal, exercising authority in matters that are the true concern of the school: teaching and learning.

By all means, the new teacher should get to know the Stern Parent officials and give them all the support possible. Nobody will appreciate it more, and nobody is in a better position to return favors.

Now it's time to discuss specific classroom situations that demand action on the part of the teacher. They range from minor occurrences encountered daily (borrowing pencils) to problems that may take place in his classroom once every five years or never (physical violence).

CLASSROOM BUZZ

As prevalent as the common cold and twice as hard to combat is a phenomenon we'll call "classroom buzz." A group of compulsive adolescent chatterers can buzz a teacher right out of business.

Classroom buzz is made up of one part necessary student conversation ("May I borrow your study guide for a minute?") and four parts unnecessary student conversation ("Who was that chick with Marilyn in the hall?") It's unfortunate that the buzz problem sometimes forces the teacher to prohibit the good along with the bad.

One classroom rule must be maintained at all times, no matter what: When the teacher is on his feet ready to talk, everybody else stops talking and listens. Not almost everybody, *everybody*.

The teacher does not begin until every eye is upon him. (He returns this courtesy by disciplining himself in what he says. He tries not to bore his students to jelly by explaining in detail how he taught his infant daughter to say "da-da," or by rhapsodizing about the world as it was when he was a boy.)

Combat classroom buzz by using all of the class time, every last bit of it. Keep the students working until a minute or two before the bell rings. Allow only as much time as necessary for finding the page in the text, completing the exercise, handing in the papers, and so on.

As exasperating as such busywork may be to the teacher, most schools expect the roll to be checked every period. In a departmentalized school, alas, such a procedure is necessary for controlling truancy. The rigamarole of absence slips must be attended to, the gradebook marked, and the names of students absent from class sent to the office. In our age of automation, it seems a rather flagrant waste of teacher time, but there it is.

Don't call roll; use your seating charts. Try to conduct the roll-checking operation while the students are at work. It is of no educational advantage whatever for students to listen to their classmates saying "here," one by one. It is very boring, and classroom buzz takes over in no time.

The buzz situation is hopeless only when the teacher isn't aware there is a problem. If he conducts classroom lectures and other activities against a constant undercurrent of student talking, he comes to accept this noise as the normal condition of the classroom, as people who live in cities accept street noise. He

ut realizing it, he raises his voice in
le is comfortable in his illusion that
few of his students actually hear a
rs, year after year, why it is that
d students and he gets all the poor

CLASSK⌐

Students will ask to borrow pencils, pens, textbooks, and—
occasionally—small amounts of money from you. Fine. Give
them what they ask for but be sure you get it back. There's an
unorthodox but effective way to insure that you will. Insist on
collateral. (Bankers do it, why shouldn't you?) Collateral may be
a ring, a watch, or the student's house keys —or even a shoe if
he has nothing else. It must be an article the student won't be
likely to leave unclaimed.

Be ready for the students who will come to your classroom
unprepared to do school work at all—no pencil, no pen, no paper,
no homework assignment, no textbook, no nothing. (See The
Timeserver, page 73.) These will be the students who are only
there at all because the attendance officer threatened to drag the
old man into court if his kid didn't go to school. All the student
wants, he'll tell you, is to leave school and get a job as soon as he's
old enough to quit legally. You'll soon find he's backed you into
a corner. Perhaps you may shrug and leave the student to flunk
as he pleases. This is an ill-advised course of action because his
idleness will soon pall and he'll generate enough trouble to upset
your teaching completely. The other alternative is to loan or give
him all the supplies he needs every time he comes to class. But
this solution quickly develops into an expensive, time-consuming
nuisance. If you find problems like this taking up too much class
time, make preparations.

Keep a supply of wastepaper from the ditto machine—sheets
that come through the machine wrinkled, too faint, or with in-
correct margins. Sometimes there are stacks of old forms the

school's not using anymore. There's nothing wrong with writing on the back of such paper. Cut the 8 ½" X 11" sheets in half on the paper cutter and keep a quarter-inch stack in some regular place in the classroom for the use of students who don't have paper. Don't put out more than that or they'll take it to make confetti for the ball game. Don't put out good notebook or ditto paper or they'll take it to use in other classes or for brothers and sisters to use at *their* schools. The no-pencil problem can be solved by keeping on hand some pencil stubs that are good enough to make a readable page but so undesirable they won't be stolen. Such stubs may be found abandoned at student desks or on the floor after the day's teaching is over. Whenever you see one, pick it up and add it to your supply.

Never make it easy for a kid to flunk. Too many students choose this path—deliberate failure—to get even with their parents, with the school, or with the world in general. They're cutting off their noses to spite their faces, of course, and the greatest service you can do these immature and not-very-wise juveniles is to put every obstacle in the way of achieving that goal. Your time will be limited and you can't manage many obstacles, but you can take care of the paper-and-pencil problem.

NOTE PASSING

Ordinarily, note passing is best ignored—but not if the delivery process demands the attention, say, of an entire row of students. Then it becomes an annoying distraction for teacher and students alike. There are several alternatives, all more or less effective:

1. You can glare. Make it clear by your facial expression that you don't expect the note passing to continue.
2. You can intercept the note, tear it up, and drop it in the wastebasket.
3. Possibly more effective than the first two is to intercept the note and do nothing at all. Slip it into your pocket or the

back of your gradebook until the end of the period. Then return it unread with no comment whatever.

SNACKS

School rules usually forbid eating in classrooms. A sure way to earn the ill will of your principal is to ignore the rule and then complain about the mice and roaches in your room. They wouldn't be there if you enforced the no-eating rule.

Students who nibble forbidden snacks in class will invariably keep the open box of candies, peanuts, or raisins in an easily accessible pocket. When your back is turned, or even when it isn't, goodie-in-pocket quickly becomes goodie-in-mouth by exercise of some of the most skillful sleight of hand since Houdini. You might teach for years and never actually witness this transfer. What gives the game away is the smell. Does your nose tell you there are peanuts around? Licorice? Look over a few shoulders. Peep into a few chest pockets. You will see the box. Ask for the box. Tell the student he may have it back at the end of the period. Give it back to him at the end of the period.

There really and truly are students who eat no breakfast at home but buy a Coke and a doughnut at school to start the day on. They'll want to eat this impromptu meal in your homeroom

or first period class. Don't permit it. Send the student outside in the hall to finish his breakfast. Tell him that henceforth he is to get to school in time to finish eating outside the classroom before the bell rings.

THE RESTROOM DODGE

"May I go to the restroom?"

"No, sorry."

"But I've got to go."

"Why didn't you go before you came to class?"

"I didn't have time."

"Well, the bell will ring in twenty minutes or so and you'll have time then. If you'll remind me, I'll dismiss you a few minutes early."

You'll say this to a dozen students before you happen across one who remembers to remind you.

"But I can't wait. I've got to go *now.*"

When a student is suffering from stomach cramps, or when a female student is in sudden monthly distress, you'll know it. In the first instance, there's a funny pinched look around the mouth, and in both cases students have a bad case of jitters for fear the emergency might overtake them. It isn't hard to spot genuine victims. Let the jittery student go and don't argue.

You'll find you need to hold the line, though, against the student who simply becomes bored in class and wants to walk around for a little fresh air, who wants to smoke a cigarette, or who has made a date to meet the boyfriend by the water fountain. In all secondary schools, classes change every hour or so, with five- or ten-minute breaks between each class. It is absurd for any student to maintain the fiction that nature's calls can't be attended to during these intervals. Even students with bona fide bladder trouble don't need more time than that!

HOW FRESH?

The line that divides cheeky familiarity from insolence is a fine one. An exchange such as "Larry, is this your paper? You forgot to put your name on it." "Big deal!" must be taken in context with your relationship with that particular pupil at that particular time. A remark like this may express no ill will whatever. On the contrary, the student may be telling you in his own rather awkward way that he thinks you're A-okay, a member of the team. But if the retort comes, say, on the heels of your reproof for the student's misbehavior, he is expressing contempt for you. Glare at him and tell him his answer is inappropriate.

Sometimes friendly banter is used to disguise a direct challenge to your authority. "Fred, stop talking now and get to work." "I ain't ready yet." No matter how friendly the words may sound, this student has flatly refused to obey you. React accordingly. "Who asked if you were ready? Get to work." Don't smile.

CHEATING

There will be plenty of cheating, unfortunately, but there are several ways to discourage it.

1. All the time the students are taking an important test, be on your feet walking around the room—not through the middle of it, mind you, but around the periphery, looking in. Be alert for unauthorized papers of any kind; "tattooed" wrists

and arms; and any unusual interest in shoes, cuffs, handbags, or wallets. Keep an especially close eye on the student who is keeping an especially close eye on you.

2. Let students know well in advance that anyone caught cheating on a test will fail the test. Stick to it, even if it's your pet-of-the-moment you must flunk and it nearly kills you to do it.

3. It's easy to prepare crib sheets for rote memory tests but hard to prepare them for tests of overall comprehension. Therefore, construct your tests with as much of the latter ingredient as possible. Ask "Why did . . .?" questions rather than "When did . . .?" or "Who did . . .?" questions.

4. Never give a test twice in exactly the same way. If you're giving the same test all day long to five different classes, change one section of it slightly. Select a different topic for an essay question for each class, or give different classes the same questions in a different sequence.

5. Don't pass out the test sheets until each desk is cleared of everything but pencil or pen.

6. Five or six times during the year, arrange to have your students write a few paragraphs or a short essay in class. Collect the papers that same day and hold them as reference samples. Should the need arise later, you can say, "Dennis, your homework assignments don't match the work you do in class. Why?" Then confront him with both papers.

7. When you discover that answers have been written into books on the classroom shelves or in school-issued books, don't waste several hours of your good time erasing them. Instead, write in more answers of your own, all wrong. Warn the students that you did this.

8. Guard your answer keys with your life.

9. Guard your gradebook with your life, especially if you are teaching college-prep students.

KEEPING TRACK OF SCHOOL PROPERTY

A dreary but necessary job the teacher must cope with is keeping track of school-provided textbooks, supplementary books on permanent loan to the classroom, lab equipment, art supplies, and shop tools. A fully equipped classroom costs between $50,000 and $100,000. Ordinary wear and tear gobble up a large hunk of that investment every year. If, in addition, little hunks of it walk out the door daily and never come back, before long there won't be enough district money left to keep teachers' salaries up with the cost-of-living index—and we don't want that to happen, do we?

The best defense a teacher has against students with taking ways is to know what is in his room. If certain items are *not* in his room, he needs to know who has them, how long they have been out of the room, and when they are due back. And he has to see to it that they *get* back.

Keep a sign-out list. A clipboard is fine. There should be a column for sign-out date, item, name of student, date due back, and check-in. All books should be numbered, and this number should be recorded on the sign-out sheet along with the title. This is especially important where several identical items of equipment are available in the classroom. When you are numbering books and equipment, don't put the number on gummed stickers that can easily be pulled off. Affix a steel tag or mark each item with a felt pen.

It's as important to insist that students sign borrowed items back in again as it is to insist they sign them out. And if the equipment is valuable, demand that the student bring the item to you so you can check it in personally. Otherwise, three days later you will ask him about it and he'll say, "I brought it back yesterday." If he can find the item with its identifying number in the room to prove he returned it, fine. But if he isn't able to, you are checkmated. Did he really bring it back? Did someone else walk off with it? Insist that a valuable article is not considered "checked in" at all unless you check it in personally and put it back in its accustomed place. And what if the student doesn't return something he has signed out? Many won't. Then you nag (see the following section).

COLLECTING DEBTS

Like the embezzler who intends to pay the money back but doesn't, there are students who intend to return the book, pay for the tickets they checked out to sell, pay back the dollar they borrowed from the teacher, pay for the dress pattern ordered in home economics class, pay for the school photographs or whatever, but don't. Elementary schools have recourse to the parents in these stituations. Secondary schools, being more interested in developing personal responsibility in young adults, hound them for the money. There is no more cheerless task. It runs something like this:

Day 1: "Some of the students in our home room have turned in their picture money or the photographs they don't want to buy, but I still do not have envelopes from the following students: Avalon, Babson, Broderic, Chisholm, Davis, Dawson, Ghilarducci, Greathouse, Hannon, Livermore, Roberts, Strum, Thomas, Trimble, Westover, White, and Yarbrough. Will you people whose names I read make it a point either to bring your photographs back or bring your money tomorrow?"

Day 2: "Some of you still haven't settled up for your photographs. I want to see the following people: Avalon, Broderic, Chisholm, Davis, Dawson, Ghilarducci, Hannon, Livermore, Roberts, Thomas, Trimble, Westover, and Yarbrough.

"All right, Avalon, what's with you? Where are your pictures?"

"I guess I lost 'em."

"Have you looked for them at home?"

"Naw."

"You owe the photographer $2.50. When will you have the money?"

"I dunno. Pa don't get paid till next Wednesday."

"Next Wednesday. Let's see, that's October 7th. He gets paid October 7th, so you should have the money the next day, October 8th. Will you write that date down here beside your name?" (That will help him remember it.) "And initial it, please. Thank you. I'll expect your money then. In the meantime, why don't you look around at home and see if you can't find them ... Broderic?"

"They're in my locker."

"What are they doing there?"

"I never took 'em home."

"Why not?"

"They was lousy."

"You never intended to buy any?"

"Lord, no."

"I wonder why you didn't turn them in three days ago?"

"I forgot."

"Go to your locker and get them now ... Chisholm?"

"I ain't got enough money to pay you now."

"How much money do you have now?"

"Only a buck and my lunch money."

"Your parents gave you the $2.50 and you spent $1.50 of it?"

"Naw. A guy stole it off me."

"Tell me about it."

"It was in P. E. My billfold was lying there and I came back and he was the only one in the room."

"When do you have P. E.?"

"Second period."

"You were here in homeroom first thing that morning with the $2.50 for the photographs before you even went to P. E. Why didn't you give me the money for your pictures while you had it?"

"I dunno." (The teacher begins to suspect that it wasn't stolen at all. He probably lost it in a crap game.)

"You'll have to ask your parents for the rest of the money or get a job and earn it."

"I can't ask them."

"If you don't pay, the school will ask them. How would you rather have them find out, from you or from us?"

"From me."

"In the meantime, pay the dollar you have. Can you bring the rest tomorrow?"

"I'll try."

"Don't try. Do it. Write tomorrow's date down here beside your name and initial it."

The bell rings, homeroom period is over, and you have not yet had a chance to talk to Davis, Dawson, Hannon, Livermore, Roberts, Thomas, Westover, or Yarbrough. Ghilarducci and Trimble are absent. Broderic has not yet returned from his locker.

Day 3: Broderic brings his photographs from his locker. Westover brings in his money. Chisholm has dug up $1.50 from somewhere—maybe he won it back in another crap game. Don't ask. Hannon volunteers that he will have his money on Friday. You interrogate Davis, Hannon, and Ghilarducci, who is back. Dawson and Trimble are absent.

Day 4: You collect from Davis. Dawson returns with her money. Ghilarducci and Trimble are absent. You talk to Livermore, Roberts, Thomas, and Yarbrough.

Day 5: Hannon and Yarbrough bring in money and photographs, respectively. Although Thomas promised to pay, he hasn't yet, so you talk to him again. Ghilarducci and Trimble are absent.

Day 6: Avalon's father has been paid, and Avalon brings his $2.50. Livermore has made arrangements to work his money out at $1.00 per week in the cafeteria. Roberts returns his photographs, which his mother discovered under his books when she cleaned his bedroom. You talk to Thomas again, who is still giving you promises and that's all. You have received a notice that Trimble has been suspended from school. Ghilarducci is absent.

Day 7: Thomas has now promised to have his money on four successive days, but still hasn't produced it. You turn in both his name and Ghilarducci's to the vice principal, who will also take over with Livermore. That finishes up the picture money until next year.

There aren't many ways out of this collection situation. It's true that with something like the photographs you can operate on a cash-and-carry basis, especially with students who have proven themselves poor credit risks before. However, in other situations, that is not practical. Suppose, for example, that everybody is selling peanuts to raise some money for band uniforms. Very few of the students' neighbors, brothers, or even mothers are going to give up any money for the peanuts until they actually see the peanuts. After all, they know the kids even better than you do! So if you refuse to part with the merchandise until you get the money from the students, your homeroom won't sell enough peanuts to sprinkle on a sundae; and when they put the sales figures up on the big chart in the hall, your homeroom will be the lowest, the kids will mope, and the principal will seem curiously aloof in your presence.

So you're damned if you do and damned if you don't.

THE PEP RALLY

There are up days and down days in the pulsing life of a school. Monday is depressive; Friday is manic. The Friday before a vacation is hypermanic. So are the classes immediately preceding a pep rally or a school assembly.

Because of the competition for the students' attention, it's a temptation to throw away these times and go through the motions of teaching in a wooden and unenthusiastic way, or perhaps have "supervised study" and not teach at all.

Resist this temptation. The pep rallies and assemblies are the head on the beer—morale raisers and school-spirit builders. Your students are in school for what goes on in class. If you compromise this position, you are letting down both your students and your school. Try to time your best, not your worst, lesson plans for assembly days. Wear your smartest outfit that day, your brightest smile, and plan your most exciting presentation.

UNWED MOTHERS

If a female student turns up pregnant, the new teacher is unlikely to hear about it, although some of the more experienced teachers might. The unwed-mother problem will be handled by the counselor or by the dean of girls and will mercifully be kept as quiet as possible to protect the girl. However, the new teacher needs to be reminded that such misfortunes do indeed befall young girls—the guesstimate is a million a year, nationwide—and that the young mothers run the gamut from the female rebel who deliberately gets pregnant in order to humiliate her parents to the helpless victim of rape by an incestuous uncle. The new teacher may never know the facts behind the case and will be in no position to moralize. So don't.

How can you tell if a girl in your class is pregnant? She may tell you, of course, but that isn't likely. There will be a clue if her schoolwork suddenly deteriorates. She may avoid your glance, come to class with eyes puffy from weeping, and develop a taste for loose shirts and tunics. Ignore it all and treat the girl exactly as though nothing is the matter. Don't pry. Instead, have a private talk with the girl's counselor and report what you have observed in class. The counselor will take it from there. If there is an abortion or if the infant is put up for adoption—whatever, the situation will be made easier for the girl by the teacher's silence.

Court decisions within the last few years have changed school policies regarding pregnant students, and it's high time. Formerly, any expectant mother, married or not, was compelled to withdraw from classes until after the baby arrived. In 1971, a Massachusetts case, *Ordway* v. *Hargraves*, was resolved in favor of the student: "It would seem beyond argument that the right to receive a public school education is a basic personal right or liberty. Consequently, the burden of justifying any school rule or regulation limiting or terminating that right is on the school authorities."

But real problems may arise if the girl remains in classes with the other students. She may be ridiculed and taunted by her classmates to such an extent that she goes home every afternoon in tears—certainly not the most wholesome situation for a mother-to-be. Or indignant parents may protest and demand that their unpregnant sons and daughters not be exposed to the moral taint (although the known father of the baby may continue to attend his regular classes, causing nary a murmur!).

Many school districts maintain special facilities where unwed mothers may continue their schooling while at the same time receiving training in child care. Others have programs where the girls may study at home or attend adult classes at night. The teacher's cooperation may be required in one way or another. Should the girl appear at your classroom door to pick up her report card or class assignments, it won't cost you a cent to give her an encouraging smile and a good luck wish, and she may treasure that moment for months to come. Avoid all editorial comment.

THE POTENTIAL SUICIDE

Sometime in the first year or two of teaching, a student in one of your classes—or perhaps a member of a school club you're sponsoring—may startle you with a remark like, "My parents don't care if I'm dead or alive." Warning bells should ring, because that's exactly what you've heard—a warning.

The cruelest thing you can do is dismiss such a statement as adolescent histrionics. Yes, the remark *could* reflect nothing more important than a temporary fit of the blues, the aftermath of a squabble the student had with his parents the night before. It could also be a signal of the chronic despair of the potential suicide.

Suicide has moved up to the third most common cause of death among young people age 15 to 24 and the incidence continues to rise. Every big high school will have at least one suicide a year, plus other "automobile accident" and "drug overdose" cases, fatal or not, where suicide is suspected. The problem is not one the teacher can shrug off.

It's sad that the myths about suicide linger on even though research has exploded the most popular ones. Victims may or may not give previous warning of their intentions. They may or may not be outstandingly intelligent or creative. Once having tried and failed, they may or may not try again. They may be boys or girls, good students or poor students, mature or childish, careful or bungling planners of the act. Suicide is almost never a product of the weather or "the mess the world is in," but may often be triggered by divorce or a death in the family. Suicide is neither shameful nor absurd. It is what happens when a despairing individual decides that his life is no longer worth living. And there is no more tragic human condition.

The new teacher may find it hard to believe, but there really are parents who don't care if their children are alive or dead. The children recognize the rejection and feel themselves betrayed or, worse, abandoned. The emotions welling up within these unfortunate young people are far more destructive, for example, than the temporary grief at losing an adolescent lover, the Romeo and Juliet story to the contrary notwithstanding. The future may bring new lovers, but when a youngster's parents reject him, he can scarcely scout around for a new set. Not ever. He is emotionally bankrupt.

"My parents don't care if I'm dead or alive" signals intense distress and your response should acknowledge the pain beneath the words. Ask, "Why do you say that?" "Hasn't there been a time in the past when you felt that your parents loved you?" "Do you have an aunt or uncle you can talk to? Grandparents?"

The answers may all be "no." Ask among the other teachers to find a clergyman who is especially gifted with young people and recommend that your student go to see him. Better still, take him yourself. Or maybe an encounter group would help. A secret Suicides Anonymous in your school might have a record of success similar to Alcoholics Anonymous.

In extremes, emphasize the future: "Sometimes we are born into the world with crushing burdens to carry, but that doesn't mean that our lives must be crippled because of them. Before long you'll be grown and will have your own family. Think what satisfaction you'll feel in giving your children the love you feel you're missing now."

WIT'S END

Someday you will draw a class that will make you wish you'd stayed on shore and cut bait. In this class there will be a higher proportion than usual of compulsive showoffs, authority challengers, big talkers, and grandstanders. Typically, it will be a big class of forty or more. In spite of doing the best teaching you know how to do, it will be impossible to get this class to pursue a discussion, watch a film, or work on a project without disintegrating into wrangling, joking, chalk-throwing, shoving disorder.

You'll want to turn in your resignation—but don't. Instead, cut your presentations before the class to a minimum. Plan the whole period, every day, for seatwork of some kind for this class. There will be no films, no phonograph records, no class discussions, and no oral reports. The schoolwork for that class will consist of reading and written work—that the students will do alone, at their desks. This will give you a ton of papers to grade. Don't grade them all. Take a few at random; check them and return them the next day. (By using irregular reinforcement schedules, no student ever knows when his paper will be checked. More effective than checking every paper, anyway.)

While students are working at their desk, patrol the room. Walk. No student is to leave his seat without permission, even to

sharpen a pencil. Don't talk aloud yourself and don't allow the students to do so. Hold whispered conversations with them at their seats about their work.

Don't make a point of this shift to seatwork. Don't comment. Just do it. Before long, students in this class will compare notes with students of your other classes and discover they're missing out on the goodies.

"Why didn't *we* get to see the film yesterday?"

"You can't handle it. A teacher must adapt his lesson plans to the needs of the students. When the students are mature enough,

the teacher can do many different things—show films, have de-
bates, things like that."

"You don't think we're mature? Is that it?"

There will be squawks, grumbling, cries of "foul." When the
protests become loud enough, it's time for your coup.

"Would you like me to show you a film tomorrow? I'll show
you what I mean."

The day you show the film, have a little surprise in store for
your students. Have a tape recorder and an hour's worth of blank
tape in the room. Tell the class that you are going to use it to
collect evidence that will prove for once and all that they are
lacking in maturity. If you've played your cards right, they'll
show you (and have the tape to prove it) that you're wrong.

VANDALISM

One afternoon after the students have gone, while making your
final check of the room before going home yourself, you will
suddenly be aware of a Playboy-type picture carved on one of
the students' desks. You'll wonder how long it's been there and
which little monster did it. Well, the little monster who did it is
the one who was sitting there. Consult your seating charts.

There are six periods in the school day, which gives you at least
six different suspects—maybe. If the desks aren't nailed down, the
carved one could have been moved from another location while
you were on duty in the hall.

You may become involved in a day or two of private questioning before you locate the artist. Remember, the students who
were seated in that part of the room won't fink and tell you who
did it. But they'll tell you who *didn't* do it, and you can discover
the culprit by the process of elimination.

Once you have unearthed your Michelangelo, get the shop
teacher to supply you with sandpaper, stain, and varnish and
teach the culprit how furniture is refinished after school. If he
rides a school bus, have him come during the noon hour.

Readers familiar with Skinnerian psychology will detect the booby trap in this procedure. The boy or girl hostile enough to carve on furniture may feel rewarded, not punished, by the annoyance he causes the teacher. With such pleasurable reinforcement, he is likely to repeat the offense. But in this case, justice must outweigh Skinner. If a student damages public property, he must be compelled to repair the damage—if, indeed, it can be repaired. It's possible to at least accommodate Skinner by shifting the focus of the situation. The "punishment" aspect can be abandoned once the teacher and the student are alone with the job. The session then becomes a matter-of-fact teaching-learning situation in which the student successfully learns something constructive and is commended for having done a good job. This way, the pleasure the student derives from being the center of the teacher's attention is not in witnessing a pyrotechinical display of the teacher's anger, but in assuming his proper role as a student and in succeeding as a student.

Most state laws stipulate that the student's parents are liable for damage to school property. If the mutilation is so extensive that a professional is required to fix it, the vice principal should be asked to have a look before anything is said to the student. Whether the damage is extensive or not, you may be asked to file a written report about it.

Vandalism is most apt to occur at either extreme of the discipline spectrum—in the overly permissive or the overly authoritarian classroom. Find the classroom style that's right for you somewhere in the middle.

THEFT

If an article of value ($5 or more) or money ($2 or more) has been stolen from your classroom, say and do nothing until you get somebody else—preferably the vice principal—in the room with you. Don't let anyone leave but the victim, whom you send for help.

There are several reasons why you shouldn't handle matters like this alone, the main one being that you don't have eyes in the back of your head. Another reason is that if an expensive article is at stake the parents must be notified and the vice principal needs to be able to talk to them from firsthand evidence. Another reason is that he will have experience in dealing with such incidents. He will know the students and their shortcomings so well from years past that he will have narrowed your list of suspects to three or four before he arrives at your door. Students who have made trouble in the past, alas, tend to make trouble in the present and future.

When the vice principal or another teacher has arrived on the scene, line the students up against the wall and have them empty their pockets and purses on the desks. Watch the entire group while the vice principal goes from student to student, or vice versa. If you try to make this student-by-student search on your own, the hot item can be disposed of behind your back—hidden in a notebook, shoe, coat pocket, etc. Don't be so naive as to expect the "good" students to squeal on the "bad" ones. According to the teen-age code, adults must spear their own fish or go hungry.

If and when the missing article is found, the offending student is escorted to the office. There, the vice principal takes over. If it's money, two or three students in the group may be carrying more than would normally be expected. They are asked to stand to one side. All of them but one will have explanations that can be verified by telephone calls to their parents. But one won't, unless his parents cover for him. Sometimes this happens, too.

Suppose money disappears and the theft isn't discovered until after the students have left the room? Notify the vice principal at once.

In the matter of school thefts, there is always an important factor working for the members of the school staff trying to find the culprit and against the culprit himself. The motive behind virtually any theft is the desire for status. The thief wants to have a finer jacket, a more handsome watch, or to spend more money on snacks. Since the very friends he wants to impress are there, in the school, mingling hourly with the same persons who are out to nail his hide to the wall, he can't very well attract the attention of one without also attracting the attention of the others. The kid can't resist flashing around whatever it was he stole; the wrong people see him, and *zap!* Many outside as well as inside crimes are solved this way. The Sharp Dresser might be arrayed in the take from last week's pawnshop burglary, and the Big Spender may be spreading the benefits of a recent service station heist. As pointed out previously, the vice principal is in close touch with the police at all times.

Within a few months, you'll get to know all your students so well you'll notice unusually flashy items of clothing, jewelry, etc., that turn up unexpectedly in their possession. Don't wonder about them in silence. Ask where they came from. "Dad bought it for me in L. A." "Yesterday was my birthday." Responses such as these are fine. The four answers that should set bells ringing are:

1. "I found it." Too often, Student A casts covetous eyes upon an especially attractive item brought to school by Student B. He bides his time, waiting for Student B to walk away from it

momentarily so he can "find" it. Student B may put down his things, walk across the room to get a book, and return to discover someone has "found" the article that was on his desk when he left. Student B doesn't know this, of course. All that Student B knows is that it's gone. (There's another "I found it" gimmick that the teacher himself can easily forestall. Let's say the bell rings at the end of Period 1 and the class members leave. Student A wanders out with her classmates, absentmindedly leaving behind the tooled leather make-up case she got for Christmas. Enter second period class. Student B spots the make-up case at the vacant desk, quietly appropriates it, and leaves with it at the end of Period 2. At noon, Student A reappears, weeping, and asks if her make-up case was found. It wasn't, but it could have been. A quick look around after each class leaves can prevent thefts of this kind.)

2. "I borrowed it." In secondary schools, where a student may know the combinations to several friends' lockers as well as his own, the temptation to "borrow" an article without the knowledge of the owner is sometimes irresistable.

3. "Louise and I traded." Technically innocent theft can occur when Student A trades her $3.95 red woolly sweater to Student B for Student B's $49.95 imported cashmere jacket. Though the swap may be fair in the eyes of both students, it definitely will not be fair in the eyes of Student B's parents.

4. "Marian sold it to me." Student B's parents aren't going to be any happier if their daughter sells the cashmere jacket to a fellow student for fifty cents than they'll be about a swap. But the money factor here is a little different. As has been said elsewhere, students are people. Like people everywhere, they are forever getting themselves into jams about money. Student B's parents have given her the money to pay her club dues at school. She has frittered it away on candy and potato chips for herself and her friends. The deadline arrives for paying the club dues. To forego the club is unthinkable; all her friends are in it. She dares

not confess her plight to her parents and face their anger, so she liquidates some of her assets at a fraction of their true value and tells her parents the articles were "stolen" or "lost." Well, in a sense they were.

In all four cases listed above, the thing to do is write down all the information you can get and turn it over to the vice principal. Five will get you ten the parents will phone wanting to know what kind of school you're running over there. (They always want to know what kind of school you're running over there.) The vice principal will appreciate having the information readily available.

You will note the emphasis on preventive action throughout this chapter. Teaching, not policing and crime detection, is the top-priority business of the school. The more minutes you devote to crime prevention, the more hours you'll save on crime detection. Shakedowns, searches, and interrogations are unbelievably time consuming. When a serious felony has been committed, an entire morning can disappear and still the missing article won't be found. If it is found, the parents of the offender or perhaps the juvenile authorities must be summoned to the school, and so it goes—on and on.

LOVE AND THE TEACHER

Nearly all students, at one time or another in their school lives, get a crush on a teacher. Sooner or later, a student will get a crush on you. When this happens, you'll know it. The onset is as obvious as a skunk in the room. The kid looks ill, hangs around all the time, and leaps to do your bidding. Pleasant though this may be in some cases, it isn't normal. The teacher should gently ease the student over his crisis so there will be as little traumatic aftereffect as possible.

There are a number of ways to accomplish this. If you have a wife, say nice things about her frequently. A husband, ditto. Keep framed pictures of the kiddies on your desk. If you have none of these assets, invent a mythical true love from another city to whom you are very devoted. This person phones you long distance and possesses unusually fine talents, intellect, and charm, all of which you happen to mention in class or to groups of your students out of class.

If you are past thirty, you can say things like "When I was a little boy, Grandfather took me to hear Lincoln at Gettysburg, bla bla bla." Talk about your pills, your allergies, your diet; bumble around a little. Use 1930's slang, or to kill even the most ardent puppy love, use 1970's slang like somebody who grew up in the 1930's and is trying hard.

So much for the student who has a crush on the teacher. There is also the teacher who gets a crush on the student. Many generalizations are risky, but this one isn't: A teacher should never, never, *never* allow himself (or herself) to become physically attracted to *any* student.

To consciously yield to such a temptation is to invite involvement in situations that are unethical, unprofessional, and insane. To yield unconsciously is worse. The band director invites the talented little blonde flutist to come after school for extra coaching alone in the bandroom. ("That girl has a real concert-grade talent if only I can develop it.") The faculty sponsor of the school newspaper works with the brilliant and lovely editor until long after dark to get out the next issue of the paper. ("Linda and I can get more done alone in five minutes than we can with all those kids in two hours.") The math teacher undertakes psychotherapy with his nymphomaniac, straight-F student. ("She needs help.")

Men aren't the only ones who are subject to this kind of poor judgment. The female teacher who tells dirty jokes to her male students, who can't resist stroking hard young biceps, is paying a high price in prestige for her camaraderie.

The aftertaste is bitter. Once established in the minds of parents at home, a reputation for lechery is still alive and kicking long after the teacher has become wiser.

Male teachers are fair game for either the nervous female student who thinks she is being pursued and isn't, or for the aggressive female who consciously wishes to be pursued but isn't.

The nervous female invents things. "Mr. Smith has been making passes at me for a month. If he doesn't stop, I'm going to tell my father." Her entire stock of evidence might amount to the fact that Mr. Smith moved her to the front row (so she wouldn't talk so much), and one day when she was examining a runner that unexpectedly popped just above her knee, she glanced up and noticed that Mr. Smith's face was pink (because he was stifling a sneeze). From this meager lode of reality, her imagination will mine leers, intimate caresses, and whispered invitations.

Girls with many friends of both sexes don't do this kind of thing. Usually, it's the inhibited loner who turns a male teacher's simple request into a lewd proposition.

The aggressive female is different. She knows what she wants —to seduce that attractive man—and she arranges things so she'll be likely to get what she's after. The male teacher may be unaware of what is in her mind until he finds himself in a nightmarish *tête-à-tête* with her. She may begin to fondle him or undress. "Alone at last," she breathes in his ear. He may stammer in bewilderment or bellow in anger, depending on his temperament and the degree of his indignation. In either case, the fat is in the fire. In no time at all, he is learning once again about the fury of a woman scorned.

Several days later, in a hearing before the school board or in a courtroom, the teacher's fate will rest on this girl's histrionic talent. Bolstered by her own rage and hurt feelings at being rejected, she will by that time have come to believe her own lies, and her histrionic talent will be impressive indeed. And who, other than the teacher himself, will know that she's lying?

When it comes to School Sex, two things will do the teacher in: privacy and time. If there is no privacy, there is no opportunity for a student to force improper issues herself or to claim the teacher forced them. If curriculum or counseling demands are such that a teacher must be alone with a student, the classroom or office door should be open. Or, if the hall is deserted, the interview might be conducted during a stroll to the office. If the teacher furnishes school-to-home transportation after the club meeting, a student of the same, not the opposite, sex, should be taken home last.

Of supreme importance is the need to act quickly when, having inadvertently given the student the opportunity, the teacher realizes he is being approached too familiarly. "No! No! Please don't tell anyone. Dear God! Please don't tell anyone. My father will beat me! He'll call me a tramp and kick me out of the house! It won't happen again, I swear!" All such hysterical pleas, promises, and explanations must be ignored. The teacher's career—not only his job at that particular school, you understand, his career as an educator—is in jeopardy. He should summon the principal, the vice principal, the dean of boys, the dean of girls, the counselor, the school nurse, another teacher or teachers, any or all secretaries, the police, the fire department, the girl's parents, the juvenile authorities, or the S.P.C.A. He desperately needs witnesses there, on the spot, at that time, to have the thing out in the open before the student has a chance to invent a story that will put her in a more flattering light.

Even then, there will be distortions of the truth. ("He grabbed me by the shoulder.") But they will be as sheerest gauze compared with the elaborate tapestry of false charges the teacher will face if a third party isn't brought in until a week later, a day later, or even an hour later. ("He ripped my clothes off and said if I didn't do what he wanted, he'd see that I never got my high school diploma and neither would my kid brother.")

Throughout the entire episode, the teacher's ablest defender and advisor will be his principal. Experience and a cool head are needed, and the principal will be more likely than anybody else to have both. It will be the principal's intention to keep his school free of scandal if at all possible. He will be reluctant to believe privately, and even more reluctant to admit publicly, that there are persons on his staff who are capable of unethical conduct. He will wish to discourage malicious attacks on male members of the school staff (including himself) by oversexed female students. He will also be loath to hire and break in a new teacher in the middle of the school year.

VIOLENCE

More rare than the sex things will be the occasion when you are done bodily harm by a student or students. In most of America's schools, you can forget this threat. It won't come up. In schools where there has been a history of such incidents, the experience of other teachers or of the principal will be valuable to you. There may be a uniformed policeman on duty at all times, and there may be a regular school procedure to follow in case you are jumped by a group of students. State laws enter into the situation. It isn't a matter of simple self-defense, as though you were attacked in a bar or on the street by other adults. These are juveniles. You have been entrusted with their care, and special laws apply—different laws in different states. Better ask.

Many classrooms are equipped with a two-way intercom system. Teachers are often suspicious of this equipment because it enables administrators to listen in on their classes at any time and they feel they are being spied upon. But there is another side of the coin; the equipment is there to protect the teacher in an emergency. When you need help, buzz the office.

Another thorny but extremely rare problem is the student who becomes loud and abusive, shouting epithets and obscenities at the teacher. He won't shut up and he won't get out. What do you do? Buzz the office or send a student for help. You may not need to. If the student is loud enough, teachers in adjoining classrooms will come to your aid and help remove him bodily, if necessary. If a student has lost control to such a point you simply don't know what he will do, don't walk out and leave your other students at his mercy. If you're afraid he might carve you up, there is an equal possibility that he may carve them up. Summon help, but stay there.

Both in the sex matter and in the case of violence in the classroom, it is to the teacher's interest to put himself in the hands of his principal, tell him exactly what happened, and do exactly what he says. The principal will probably tell the teacher not to discuss the matter with anyone else. That's the best advice of all. Let him handle it.

DRUGS

Another time to get help as soon as possible is when you suspect that a student is stoned. Don't try to guess from his

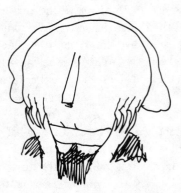

behavior what drug he's taken because you can't tell. He may have sneaked a joint in the restroom or gulped down a couple of bennies on the way to class. With either drug (or with a double martini, for that matter) he might become nervously overtalkative or groggily undertalkative depending on recent events, his personality, and his physical condition.

Beware of false accusations that could cause more mischief

than they're worth. If a student seems excited or depressed, who knows?—perhaps he's in love. If the attack seems minor, assume that it's innocent and handle it accordingly.

But if the behavior is so erratic that the other students turn to stare and comment, it's time to get the offender out of the room. What you need at this point is a trustworthy varsity halfback to steer the culprit to the nurse's office and notify the vice principal for you. It's too bad that there aren't enough reliable jocks to supply every teacher with a bouncer, but there aren't, so you'll probably end up taking your suspected drug victim to the office yourself. He (or she) may refuse to go. Don't argue. Send an S.O.S. note to the vice principal and leave the rest up to him.

A potentially dangerous situation may arise when a student passes out at his desk and can't be aroused. The student may simply be sleeping off the effects of the first Seconal pill he ever took in his life. There may be nothing wrong that a few hours' sleep won't mend, but the things that *could* be wrong are so dire that a red alert is indicated. For one thing, the student may not be reacting to drugs at all. He could be suffering a heart attack or he may have lapsed into a diabetic coma, either or which could end in tragedy if the teacher doesn't act quickly. Or if drugs are the trouble, the victim might be dying from an overdose of God-knows-what. In fact, *only* God may know what: the student himself may have no idea what was in the capsules he swallowed.

No matter. Don't take chances. Summon the nurse and/or vice principal immediately. Stretch the youngster out on the floor and loosen his clothing for easier breathing. Find out what you can from the other students. Has the kid behaved strangely in other classes? Was he absent from other classes? Has he been in a fight? Did he take drugs? If so, what?

When he arrives, the vice principal may commandeer two or three of your classmembers to carry the victim to the nurse's office. Return to your clasroom work.

What's with kids and drugs, anyway? When the first edition of this book was prepared in 1966, the author had only heard of rare cases of teen-age drug abuse and would have expected to see a live panda scaling the curtain cord before she saw a youngster on a drug trip in her own clasroom. Yet by the time the book had been in print a year, it was evident that failure to mention the drug problem left a discernible gap.

How the scene has changed! Today, instruction on drug abuse may begin as early as elementary school. High school teachers think twice before leaving an open thermos of coffee when students are around; some clown might drop LSD into it. High school officials think twice about selling soft drinks at dances for the same reason. There is such danger of spiked punch at school parties that in some cities these functions are a thing of the past.

It's become a cliche to observe that ours is a drug culture. Physicians themselves say that almost two out of three visitors to their offices have nothing physically wrong with them. Since the patients aren't sick, there's nothing the doctors can give them to make them well; instead, they take the easy way out and prescribe pills to make the patients "feel better." The result is that Mr. and Mrs. America have come to seek instant relief from fatigue, anxiety, pain, sleeplessness, depression, and feelings of inferiority through drugs. The practice sets a devastating example for the young.

High school students are well aware of adult hypocrisy on the drug question and dwell on it at length. "Mom takes uppers and downers, too, but she calls it 'medication.'" "Pot isn't as harmful as booze." "A joint won't give you lung cancer." "Doctors are the biggest pushers of all."

There's enough truth in these charges to put the unwary teacher on the defensive. The temptation is there to lecture. Don't. The only adults who seem able to talk effectively to the young about drug abuse are ex-users. Let them do it.

There's One in Every Crowd

"That kid is a pest!" says Teacher A to Teacher B. "All he wants is attention."

If Teacher A would reflect a moment, he'd realize that's all Akhnaton wanted, or Charlemagne, or Madame Curie, or Thomas Jefferson, or Buckminster Fuller. What's so bad about wanting attention? Man would have foundered in the morass of his own folly centuries ago if it hadn't been for the visionaries, revolutionaries, and plain crackpots who wanted attention and went about getting it in constructive ways.

Many of your students, unfortunately, will go about getting it in inappropriate ways. It will become part of your task not to discourage the boy who paints blue daisies on his face, but to handle him in such a way that he may one day write an award-winning film script. (Creative artists of this caliber are few and far between!)

This chapter will be devoted to a discussion of stereotypes the teacher is likely to encounter in his classes, together with suggestions for resolving the problems typically presented by them. The same convention will be observed in discussing these students as has been employed in referring to the teacher throughout this book, that is, use of the masculine gender. You should not assume that the pronoun "he" means that boys are troublemakers and girls aren't. Such is scarcely the case, although some categories are likely to be more heavily weighted toward one sex than the other.

Gigglers, for example, are usually girls, and there are possibly more female than male Transients, because they make liberal use of female problems to get out of class. On the other hand, Cliff-hanger I will nearly always be a boy, but Cliff-hanger II may more often be a girl.

Whether it's Robert or Roberta, Steve or Stephanie, however, you will meet a goodly number of the following stereotypes your first month in the classroom, and the rest before your first year is over.

THE CLOWN

Every class of twenty-five or more will have a Clown. When he misbehaves, which is frequently, he does so in such a way you are sure to catch him and punish him. As a last resort, he will even point out to you what he did wrong and plead with you to punish him!

There is a streak of masochism in his makeup. He never wins. He arranges things so he won't. He gets his kicks from losing, from being the "stupid" one in the group, the butt of all the jokes.

What he needs from you, specifically, is your good-natured jibe before he can settle down happily to work. It's not the same if you kid him in private. There must be an audience.

Insulting this kid from time to time will keep his mischief in check, but it won't help him to overcome his handicap, which, if allowed to continue, will lead him a tragic lifetime course down

Loser Lane. He can be encouraged to satisfy his need for ridicule by substituting an appropriate surrogate. In schoolwork, he might be channeled into dramatic comedy parts of the Punch and Judy genre. He should do well in English with first-person-singular narrative in which the first-person-singular is a bumpkin of outlandish proportions. Comic dance, tumbling, trampoline acts, cartooning might answer. Another character *whom he has created* must be the fall guy, thus freeing him to work for, rather than against, his own best interests.

THE WHINER

This youngster is very hard on the nerves. He is a malingerer, and usually a hypochondriac as well. He will have a bottomless reservoir of reasons why he can't do his homework, read the chapter, find something on the map, or do calisthenics. "Poor me," he says. "I am a victim of my weak constitution, bad eyes, poor education, crowded home, ill-tempered father, the welfare department, that mean teacher I had last year, lumps in my liver and so forth."

His goal is to squeeze from you every possible drop of sympathy. He may succeed for a while. He has had years of practice in sympathy-getting and has become proficient at it. You will wonder how he got that way until you meet his parents at the first P.T.A. meeting. After that, you'll know. They're that way, too.

This kid will nail you early, the first day. You are a fresh, untapped source of sympathy, and his eyes will mist over in happy anticipation. But don't go along with it. Tell him with a brisk smile that you can't do anything about his past troubles. You are there to help him learn so he may have fewer troubles in the future. If he suffers from poor health, all the more reason to study hard so he can overcome his handicap in the future when he must get a job. Do everything you can to get work of some kind out of this student. And when you get it, give him a warm smile of respect and commend him. Brush off his excuses, but never fail to commend his accomplishments. His accomplishments will probably be awful, just awful; but if he persists in his attempts to do his schoolwork, his work will improve. You must have faith that this will happen and make him have faith it will happen. What you're primarily interested in is getting him to *do* something so he'll stop bellyaching about why he *can't* do it.

You won't reform the Whiner all by yourself. Forget that. It would take far more than one teacher far more than one year to perform that miracle! But you can get him off your neck in your class. And who knows? You may actually succeed in teaching him something!

THE TIMESERVER

This fellow is a lot like the Whiner, but he presents a more complex problem. The Whiner has at least bestirred himself to get something, sympathy. As long as there's a spark, a desire for something, no matter how sick the something may be, you can direct this desire, encourage it, and perhaps come up with worthwhile results. But the Timesaver doesn't want sympathy. He doesn't want anything. He just sits there. He is an inert mass of programmed hamburger. He has been wired to get up and leave

when the bell rings and, perhaps, answer roll call, but little else. He may take a nap from time to time. He rarely talks to anyone, least of all to you. He may be in your class a month before you hear him utter a sentence.

He isn't afraid he'll flunk. On the contrary, he is quite sure he will flunk because he more often flunks than not. He has given up, and in his case it was probably the only sensible way to deal with an environment he could neither conform to nor change.

In any problem with a student, the less emotionally involved you allow yourself to become, the better off both of you will be, but particularly is this true in the case of the Timeserver. He, of all problem students, will be the most likely to infuriate you. Either that or break your heart. His disinterest in you, school, books, and education is complete and bone deep.

You need to research this student thoroughly before you make a move, so don't make any until you've asked several people about him. If there's any danger of borderline psychosis, you don't want to be the one to shove him over the line. Most of your information will come from his counselor and other teachers, but oblique questioning of a few students who know him well may also help.

Is he mentally ill? Has he been referred to the school psychoanalyst? When? Were there treatments? For how long? With what results? Is there mental illness in his family? Does he act the same way outside of school as in it? Is he this way in all classes, including P.E. and shop? If not, you've got a fighting chance. How have other teachers handled him and what were the results?

His school records in the counselor's office should indicate how long he's been the way he is. When did he become a straight-F student? If he "gave up" within the last year or so, you may still snap him out of it. If it's gone on for three or more years or if he'll soon be of legal age to quit school or both, you're licked on the education end—but you may still be able to use him as a teacher's aide in your class.

Most important of all, is his behavior truly what it appears to be—total demoralization—or is it a teacher-baiting device? It will be easy to determine this from the other teachers. Is he after peace at any price, or is he after a fight at any price? It is the answer to this question that will give you your cue in handling him.

If there is a history of mental disturbance, or even a suspicion anywhere that there might be such a condition, leave him alone. Smile at him. Perhaps once a week when the other students are working at their seats, you might quietly go to him and, in a whisper, invite him to do what the other students are doing. Don't order him; invite him.

If you're lucky and actually get some work out of this student, say to him privately, "I was glad to see you turned in a paper yesterday, Robert. I'll bet it wasn't as bad as you thought it would be. Would you like me to show you the ones you got right?" Not *wrong*, notice; right. If you only talk about the right ones, soon he'll begin to wonder on his own about the wrong ones and either ask you about them or fix them up himself. Don't gush. Phony praise is worse than none at all.

If he doesn't respond to this tack, see if you can find magazines that interest him, or books. If you have a book table at the back of the room, let him sit there regularly. Be kind to him. Put things he might like where he can find them. And leave him alone.

But suppose your research indicates that this student is merely testing you to see how much you'll put up with. More pressure is called for, and you'll have to keep applying it over a long period of time—probably for the entire year.

Oddly enough, if this student weighs 200 pounds and you weigh 110 pounds, you have an advantage. But if the student weighs 200 and you weigh 180, you have no advantage. Don't ask me why. Maybe it has something to do with roles. Little people with a lot of gumption can push big lugs around and big, muscle-bound types can push runts around and in both cases the victims love it. But when the weight balance is close enough to leave doubt about who's the "big guy" and who's the "little guy" (even with female combinations) a contest develops. If you're near the same size, don't push or shove. *Just lean gently.*

Having been forewarned on this score, you should be forewarned on another. The hardest way to handle any discipline problem is to let it develop into an eyeball-to-eyeball "you will," "I won't," "you will," "I won't," dispute. All this proves is who can yell the loudest. Anyway, whether the student will or won't shouldn't be part of the issue at all. Assume from the outset that he will; the only matter in doubt is how well and to what extent.

Once you have determined that your Timeserver is not a borderline psychotic, see to it he is supplied with a textbook next time he comes to class. He won't have one with him. Give him one from the classroom supply. You'll also have to give him paper and pencil from the classroom supply. Find the right page for him. Gently explain to him in a few words what the class is doing. Treat him as you would your invalid kid brother whom you're fond of and want to take care of. Conduct your class as usual but keep coming back to his seat to see if he needs help. "You'll need to number down the side of the page, Al. Here, let me show you." "Would you like me to read that first question for you?"

No sarcasm is called for—no nasty innuendos, no asides to the other students in the class. You are dealing with an educationally crippled student who needs a lot of help. Your solicitude will begin to hurt his pride after a while, and he'll do something on his own to get kindly old you off his back.

Check his paper for him, what there is of it, right there at his seat. Let him see what he did right and explain what he did wrong. If you gave him a grade at all it would probably have to be an F, so don't give him one. Confine your praise to a business-like "good."

Next day, repeat the routine. Teach the kid "by hand" until he's operating on his own steam. If his work continues to be so poor that he'd get F's if you gave him grades, don't give him any, ever. Explain at the office that you are tutoring this student because he has special learning problems (he does!) and you don't know what kind of grade to give him. Write "Pass" on the forms where his grades are supposed to go.

THE GIGGLER

This will be a girl. She's nervous. She's as embarrassed by her affliction as you are exasperated by it. She can no more stop her giggling than you can stop the hiccups. Have her sit in the front

row where she can't see so many male students and won't have so much to be nervous about. Have her help you with chores such as sorting papers, alphabetizing cards, and putting out the cut slips for the office girl. If the opportunity should arise, ask her advice about something and follow it.

THE PHANTOM GENIUS

Few school districts reveal scores on scholastic aptitude tests to parents. There are cases when they probably should. Tests of this kind measure the student's ability to reason, to distinguish patterns, to discriminate between shades of verbal meaning—in short, what school people rightly or wrongly call his "intelligence." The layman, without the figures before him, tends to see evidence of this quality in the wrong things, or to pay too much attention to the right things in the wrong context.

A student we'll call The Phantom Genius may be thought by his parents to be brilliant because he learned his arithmetic facts early and learned them extremely well, or because he has a large speaking vocabulary, or perhaps merely because he is the only one in his family who reads at grade level, his brothers and sisters being retarded. The student may not be brilliant at all. His teachers may consider him just an average kid with a good memory or one who gets his jollies by using big words in all the wrong places. Yet the student conducts himself with the aplomb of an intellectual giant. Why? Because his family has always told him he was an intellectual giant. They told him and told him. The kid has developed into a snob with nothing to be a snob about.

Now intellectual snobbery is bad enough when the brains and talent are there to justify it, as we shall see presently with The Derailed Genius; but when snobbery is rooted in fiction, the expected fruit will never mature. Both the student and his parents will harvest disappointment and little else.

The pattern is nearly always the same. In his schoolwork, The Phantom Genius and his parents will feel his mediocre grades are reflecting the teacher's ill will. It will never occur to them that his grades are reflecting his own mediocre performance. As he progresses through elementary to secondary school, his lack of ability will become more apparent, and his grades may sink from B's to C's. There may even be a D or two. The tension between home and school will build.

At home, The Phantom Genius is desperately clinging to his treasured status in the bosom of the family and complains bitterly of teachers who won't give him a chance, who deliberately twist things he says, who "have it in for him." When the situation can be tolerated no longer the parents march grimly to school, chip on shoulder and blood in eye. Usually, the counselor (lucky man!) will be the one who talks them out of tarring and feathering a teacher or two. He will give them the information they need to bring their expectations of their child into sharper focus, and that will just about be that. But if you have been alert to this problem, you have the power to stop it before it gets that far. Before a month has passed, The Phantom Genius' problem will become uncomfortably clear to you.

When he first enters your class, you will assume from his behavior that he is among the brighter students in the group. He will patronize the lesser lights and adopt a stance of leadership quite naturally. His role may be so skillfully played that you may be taken in by it. You simply won't believe your eyes when you grade your first test and his performance turns out to be wretched. If the next two or three weeks confirm that his performance is uniformly as poor as your first sample, invite him in for a conference. Prepare for it by collecting a large group of student papers (twenty minimum), all of which have been checked by you, all of which have the grades prominently displayed on them. Reports, tests, daily quizzes, themes, and lab reports should be included, and should represent a range from A to F in quality. Turn over the corners of the papers so the names can't be seen if you like, but this isn't absolutely necessary. Have three or four of The Phantom Genius' papers there, too.

"Gerald," you will open the interview. "Do you understand why it is you are making C's and D's in my classes?"

"No, indeed, I do not, and what's more, I ..."

"I thought perhaps you didn't. So I got some things together here that might be of interest to you."

Arrange the specimens from A papers down to F papers. Let him look and read and look and read and look some more. He will ask a few questions.

"What's so great about this paper what got a A?"

Tell him.

"My handwriting ten times improve over this'n here and you gimme a C and you give him a B. How come?"

Tell him.

When he's seen enough and is ready to go, say, "Gerald, I'd like very much to invite your parents to come to school to talk about your grades. I'll bet they're disappointed that you're not doing better in your school work, aren't they?"

"Yeah. They disappointed."

"Would you object if I phoned your mother and asked her to come to school one afternoon next week? And your father, too, if he can make it."

"Well . . . let me consult her when I gits home this afternoon and see what she say."

"All right. And will you let me know tomorrow?"

Gerald may decide to handle the matter as best he can by himself—"She say she awful preoccupied presently, can she come sometime later?" On the other hand, he might chicken out and let you do it your way—"She say she exaggerated you invite her. What day?"

If she comes, make arrangements for the counselor to be present with you at this interview. It's unwise for a new teacher to handle a parent-teacher conference alone if there is any likelihood of ill feeling. After the necessary points have been covered, you should excuse yourself and let the counselor talk to her alone.

Afterwards, if Gerald is half as bright as he pretends to be, he'll tell his parents, "I sorry I not as smart as you all thought I was," and everybody will have a good cry. A new and better day will dawn—for the family, for Gerald's teachers, and, most important of all, for Gerald himself.

There will be other cases where the solution to the problem won't be nearly this simple. Gerald's self-image is at stake. Since birth he has believed he was a Superior Person, and his terror of admitting, especially to himself, that he is just about like everybody else will lead him to resort to every known defense. Over the years, The Phantom Genius becomes an expert at cheating. He will learn the advantages of being a slow and methodical worker. ("Let me take it home and copy it over" and also correct all the mistakes.) He will learn to be sick on test days and will quickly cry foul if the teacher doesn't give him the same test for make-up that was given to the other students two days before.

It's quite possible for the problem to be so deeply rooted that the student faces severe emotional disturbance if he is forced to admit his own inadequacies. He literally *must* kid himself if he is to survive at all. To know and accept himself for what he is would require months, perhaps years, of psychotherapy, treatment the school is in no position to provide. In this case, about all the school can do is suffer along with him until he graduates. And he will, never fear. Incredible feat, but he'll wangle it.

THE DERAILED GENIUS

It gives the wrong impression to devote an entire book to troublesome adolescents and say nothing whatever about the other kind. For every teen-ager who falls in the school's liability column, there will be twenty-five middlegrounders and at least half a dozen in the asset list who are absolute jewels, without whom it's difficult to see how the school would function at all. They are the school's pacesetters, sparkplugs, and errand runners.

They enjoy sound mental as well as physical health and discipline themselves from a rich fund of common sense. They show up promptly every morning, scrubbed, co-operative, and enthusiastic, with heads chock full of dandy little ideas that work.

Many (not all) of these jewels will score in the upper brackets on the scholastic aptitude tests. Their parents are bright, too, not only about books but about everything, including the way they bring up their offspring. Typically, behavior problems are rare among these bright students, the most serious being an unbecoming tendency toward mouthiness. In college-prep groups, classroom buzz becomes classroom roar in the time it takes the papers to be passed to the front of the room. Annoying, but scarcely threatening if kept under control.

Truly bright youngsters seem to come with built-in *noblesse oblige.* It's a hallmark of the ultra-bright student that distinguishes him from the medium-bright one. They shrink, these sharpies, from using their superior minds in ways that hurt others. As a group, they tend to be remarkably free of malice themselves or the suspicion of malice in others—sometimes to the point of gullibility. They will almost never discuss their brains or spend time worrying about what is worthy of their intelligence and what isn't.

The arrogant, overbearing parvenu with an I.Q. of 140 or better is as hard to find as edelweiss on the Baja Peninsula. And that's good, because if you ever have the misfortune to draw one of these in a class, you will come to welcome him every day as you would a third degree burn. We'll call him The Derailed Genius.

The big difference between The Phantom Genius and The Derailed Genius is that the teacher, *any* teacher, is usually smarter than The Phantom Genius, whereas The Derailed Genius may match his teachers in intelligence or surpass them. Not only does the Derailed Genius know this, he never lets his teachers forget it. He uses his intelligence daily to degrade and bully them into submission.

The Derailed Genius is a loner by choice. His tastes are too refined for him to associate with his peers in the honors class; he considers them immature, even though they are often brighter than he is. School rules, he maintains, are for clods and are not to be tolerated by creative, sensitive persons of his caliber. The curriculum itself, and above all, the teachers who present it, are geared to the ordinary and cannot be expected to appeal to the extraordinary (him), even though the school may take particular pride in its college-prep curriculum. He drags his feet on school-work because he's saving himself for the superbrainy professors who await him at Harvard (or Cal, Yale, Princeton, etc.). He has been saving himself for so long, in fact, and blackmailing his teachers for grades for so long, that he is actually a very poorly educated person! He can't express either concrete ideas or abstractions on paper, much less punctuate them properly or spell the words correctly. He isn't sure if Isaac Newton was American or British, or if Shakespeare and Chaucer were contemporaries. His notions of mathematical functions and physical laws are hazy at best and totally inaccurate at worst.

When you confront The Derailed Genius with the gaps in his educational background, he will tell you he is interested in theoretical work and prefers not to clutter up his mind with the rote-learned trivia of public school education. You may wonder how he plans to get into college at all with no more preparation than he has, but then you will remember his straight A record (what teacher has dared to give him anything else?) and his truly impressive intelligence test scores.

Your imagination will stagger at the picture of this intellectual freak in a freshman class in any college or university in the land. The overwhelming temptation will be to wash your hands of him and let him flunk out of Harvard, where, with stiffer competition, he will automatically shift classifications from The Derailed Genius (somebody special) to a point even below The Phantom Genius (somebody about average).

Coping with the problem is a thorny assignment. The precautions to be observed with The Derailed Genius are identical to those observed with The Phantom Genius. The matter of ego strength must be gauged, and a talk with his counselor may be profitable. If you feel up to tangling with him and Mama (there's always Mama, I.Q. about 115), you can undertake to educate him. You may insist that he obey the same rules as the other students, turn in work of the same quality and at the same time as the other students, and be graded by the same criteria as the other students —in short, demand that he put up or shut up.

The paper routine recommended for The Phantom Genius won't work with The Derailed Genius. The Phantom Genius and his parents are willing to admit that there are such things as right and wrong answers and that the ability to write a good essay is important. The Derailed Genius and his Mama will emerge from such a session unscathed. They will insist that tests and themes measure conformity and little else. They convinced themselves long ago that his dynamic intellect far outshone that of his classmates. What they will challenge is not what grades he deserves, but your right, as a mere public servant, to teach him at all!

Don't start your campaign unless you're prepared to follow through all year. You don't need to be more intelligent than he is. After all, you're only trying to teach him what you know, and at the present time he knows considerably less than you do. You need, however, to be more stubborn than he is, and you also need a thick skin; he'll make a monkey of you every time you turn around. It will be a rough fight. Be sure you keep the principal informed about what you're doing and why. Mama will be phoning him, and phoning him, and phoning him.

THE INCUBATING GENIUS

This student is also rare, perhaps rarer than The Derailed Genius. You may teach a lifetime and see him only once or twice, or perhaps not at all. He is included here because in the event he does come along, it's so terribly important not to let him down.

He's equipped with a special kind of vision that enables him to see through phoniness, which he loathes. He's as independent as a hog on ice—a Truth Seeker and a Truth Teller whose honesty sometimes gets him in trouble with the authorities. Other than his penchant for telling the truth, he's so quiet and unassuming that you may not know he's there at all. You won't discover what a unique and amazing person he is until his written work begins to come in.

He probably won't be able to spell, either, but his choice of subject matter will dumbfound you. He'll write about things most adults don't think about, let alone adolescents. What is good, and why does good sometimes turn out to be bad? Is there anything that's important, and if so what? What are we all doing here, anyway?

He isn't being impertinent or glib. He isn't challenging you, as The Derailed Genius might be, enticing you into abstractions that are beyond your depth so he can make you look like a jackass. This student wants answers.

Well, you won't be able to supply them, so don't try. You aren't enough like The Incubating Genius for your answers to satisfy him at all. He's going to be brainier than you, more creative than you, and far, far more restless than you. The tremendously important thing you can do for him is to head him in the direction of other brainy, creative people via books. Give him Gibran to read, and Montaigne, de Tocqueville, Camus, Joyce, Plath, Santayana, Kierkegaard, Freud, Kafka, Baldwin, and Toynbee. You won't always come up with something he digs, but keep trying.

Get him to talk. How is he reacting to what he's reading? Does he disagree with the ideas of these writers? Why? If you don't have the mental or educational equipment to discuss these matters with him, for heaven's sake don't make the mistake of pretending you do. There's no need to, anyway. You'll discover he finds weaknesses in his own arguments more quickly than you would. He needs a listener. He's trying on different ideas to see how they fit. He won't find his answers, ever; but by the time he's forty, he will have settled for educated guesses, the most creative of which might very well be his own.

THE SEX SYMBOLS

Briefly, these types are overstimulated by the opposite sex. Their physicians will say they have hyperactive glands, their counselors will say they are insecure, and their peers will say they're horny. Regardless of the diagnosis, a seductively twitching, eye-rolling lass seated in the midst of half-a-dozen young

bucks can play hob with your lesson plan. Move her into the midst of half-a-dozen other girls. Use similar therapeutic procedures for the scintillating male who has gathered a giggling harem about him: break it up.

A more difficult version of this problem comes about when the student isn't soliciting attention at all, but is simply attractive, devilishly so. No matter where you move a truly lovely teen-age girl in a room half full of teen-age boys, the boys will behave like hyenas. If she is demure and feminine, it makes matters worse, not better. A handsome, slim-hipped boy who dresses and moves well can have the same effect on girls. Bury these handsome children out of sight at the back of the room. Use every stratagem you can think of to keep them there. When it's time for oral reports, schedule theirs last. Don't call on them to recite until just before the bell rings.

CLIFF-HANGER I

It's part of growing up for boys to place themselves in dangerous situations to find out if they're man enough to handle them. Girls can have babies. To prove her feminity, all a girl need do is leave everything up to Mother nature. But to prove himself a man, a boy must test muscle and wit to the utmost before he can wholly know who and what he is.

Many parents are shrewd enough to realize this, and their sons go out for school sports with their blessings—or take up such hobbies as cave exploring, scuba diving, flying, sky diving, skiing, or herpatology. Though physical risks in these pursuits may be high, the parents reason it is better for the boy to fight it out with an eight-foot anoconda and risk a lacerated arm than to race a buddy on the public highway at 125 mph and risk instant death.

The intensity of the urge to hang from cliffs without actually falling varies in degree from individual to individual. The Cliff Hanger Senior Grade wants to find out how far he can go without killing himself. He is reckless beyond the call of duty and inspires awe in the Cliff Hanger Junior Grade, who merely wants to find out how far he can go before he gets caught stealing Pop's bonded bourbon or before he breaks a leg—or before he gets kicked out of school.

The student we are considering somtimes comes to school and sometimes doesn't. He is a master at forging notes from home.

Though he cuts classes when he feels like it, which is often, he is never without an "excuse" on his return. He smokes forbidden cigarettes in the restroom, and later comes to class with a green-stained tongue from the chlorophyll gum he is careful to chew.

He has made a thorough study of the rules, classroom rules of individual teachers as well as those of the school at large, and he knows how to circumvent them. His hard-luck tales would wring tears from a golf ball, but his protestations of good will have a phony ring, as though he memorized entire paragraphs from *Boy's Life.* He plays teachers off against counselors or against each other with distortions of the truth—or downright lies.

Over the years, his sins accumulate until he arrives at a point where he isn't actually "in" school at all; he is there so seldom that he has lost track of his schoolwork and his teachers have lost track of him. From time to time he is caught; but, thanks mainly to his own skill, he hasn't yet been caught in the final transgression that will expel him. So, he isn't "out" of school, either.

This student's situation may become so interesting it provides a staple item of school gossip, both with the faculty in the lounge and the students in the cafeteria: "Has Fred gotten kicked out yet?" This adventure may go on for a couple of years. Incredibly, the kid may even get his diploma and at last prove to the world

he prevailed against formidable odds and triumphed, a man indeed!

What should the new teacher do with this character? As little as possible. Most likely, his life will already be crowded with counselors, juvenile court officers, and social workers. There are apt to be divorced parents and step-parents, brothers and sisters, step-brothers and step-sisters, and perhaps a pregnant girl or two waiting in the wings. (Typically there will be several cliffs he's hanging from simultaneously.) You will only make matters worse by interfering with his problem or by forcing unnecessary issues. Compute his grades as honestly as you know how and send them in. Note his absences and tardies and send them in. When he's there, smile at him.

Necessary issues, of course, are a different matter. Should he become angry about something in your class and swear at you, you must report the matter to the vice principal, even if it brings the house of cards crashing to the ground. But it's not likely he'll do this. What he'll do instead is *almost* give you cause to report him.

When you see the first signs that Cliff-Hanger I has sweet old you pegged as still another cliff it would be fun to hang from, go to his seat for a little exercise in communications.

"Fred," you might say, "I have talked to the other teachers about you. They don't seem to like you much."

"Yeah."

"And I've talked to the assistant principal about you. He doesn't seem to like you much, either."

"Yeah."

"They all tell me you're about to get kicked out of school. Is that right?"

"Yeah."

"All that's needed to kick you out of school is to be sent to the office just one more time by a teacher. That right?"

"Yeah."

"I see."

Fred is pretty good at communications. He will get your message.

CLIFF-HANGER II

Judged on the basis of superficial behavior alone, this student belongs with the Whiner and the Timeserver; sometimes it's easy to confuse them. Motive is the differentiating factor. The Malingerer wants a free ride, and he proposes to use your sympathy for a ticket. The Timeserver *at one time* wanted to participate in school and do well, but has resigned himself to failure and is only waiting till the calendar sets him free. Cliff-Hanger II wants the diploma, always wanted it, but never at any time saw a reason to expend more effort than absolutely necessary to get it. He hangs in the delicate balance between passing and failing. That's exactly where he wants to be. He can be shifted from one curriculum track to another like a handcar, and he will find his place *almost* at the bottom of the class.

Cliff-Hanger II is lazy. Bone lazy. It isn't a matter of blood pressure or neurosis, but of values. Physical ease is the *summum bonum*, and his tribal diety is the three-toed sloth. His achievement in class will be lower than his scholastic aptitude scores would lead you to expect. He may be slightly dull or very bright. Indeed, he might one day win a doctorate, having exercised meticulous care along the way to do only what was absolutely necessary to get it.

Typically, he will make C's and D's. When he finds his grade-point sinking to such depths that his diploma is jeopardized, he will argue with you about the mark you gave him. Whatever his grade, if you computed it correctly and there is no reason to change it other than his pleas for "another chance," refuse to change it. Do nothing beyond what is absolutely necessary (*sic!*) to give him fair grades. Your obligation ends there.

THE OPERATOR

There will be the student who apparently went through the line four times when they were passing out aggressive tendencies. This boy will become a sales executive someday and make more money in one year than you make in five. Everywhere he goes, in any situation, under any conditions whatever, he will take over. He will take over your class if you let him.

If the students all like him and willingly accept his leadership in the class, you can use him as a sort of unofficial sergeant-at-arms and things will go fairly smoothly. But you'll more often

find the other students don't like him and will resent his high-handed ways. Furthermore, you will lose the respect of these other students if you allow him to get out of line.

There is no easy way out. You will have to call him down and call him down, take him out in the hall to talk to him, and no doubt send him to the office fairly often for some moral support from the vice principal. You can squelch him for short periods, ("My teaching credential is at home in my desk. Where's yours?") but two days is about all the peace this kind of thing will buy you. Sorry.

THE TRANSIENT

In a big high school, at any given time of the morning or afternoon, you will find perhaps 3 percent of the student body not in class at all, but walking up and down the halls. Whether it's Monday or Thursday, October or May, it will almost always be the same 3 percent. They will be engaged in a variety of pursuits. This one has his teacher's permission to get notebook paper from his locker. That one is on his way to the restroom or (smelling strongly of cigarette smoke) has been to the restroom and is on his way back to class. A third, absent yesterday, has "lost" his permit to class and is on his way to the office to get a duplicate. A fourth student "has a headache" and has been excused to go to the nurse. A fifth is "going to the office to see his counselor," secure in the knowledge that his counselor is away from the school at a meeting. A sixth is cutting class because he hasn't written the report that's due today. A seventh has been summoned to the attendance office to account for the class he cut two days ago. On and on it goes.

With the exception of a few students who will be out of class on legitimate business, such as getting a book from the library or gathering information for the school paper, all of these students will be Transients, young people who have devoted years of thoughtful study and practice to the fine art of getting out of class.

Why do they want to get out of class? Because, as it is traditionally conducted, education is less a process of developing the physical, intellectual, and aesthetic talents of the young than it is a twelve-year poker game in which the intellectually able consistently hold the high cards and win and the not-so-intellectually able consistently hold the low cards and lose. For the winners, the arrangement is peachy-keen but the losers don't like it especially. They get out of class if they can.

A teacher who deals successfully with Transients must keep them in class and make class so satisfying that they no longer want out.

The first requirement is simple and demands only the stamina to say: "No, you can't be excused to go to the restroom; wait until the end of the period." "Start on your report now, so you'll have it ready when it's due next week." "Leave word in the office that you want to see your counselor and he'll send for you when he can see you."

The second requirement is harder, because it involves more than superficial things like a pretty room and movies once a week. It has to do with what you really think and feel about education. Forget for the moment what the education profs told you. Deep in your heart what do you *really* believe is the purpose of education? To award diplomas? Is the high school setup nothing but a rubber-stamping process that enables students to get into college or to get a job? If that's what you really believe, then do your Transients (and yourself) a favor and set them free to wander at will.

On the other hand, maybe you see more to education than that. A wealth of research proves that the human organism wants to learn, wants to discover new ideas—in fact, *needs* grist for the mental mill more urgently than it needs food. Give a hungry baby a bottle then turn on a music box beside his bed. He'll stop sucking to listen. Such is the compelling power of intellectual curiosity.

What are your students curious about? There are things they are itching to learn; what things? The trouble with education is that it does too much scratching where it doesn't itch, and it rubs people raw.

If your Transients can get the information they want from magazines and newspapers, forget the textbook. If they can get it from each other, that's even better—as long as you make sure it's information, not ignorance, that they're sharing.

One more comment before we leave our student stereotypes. Never resent the students who force you to do your best teaching. They'll make a pro out of you. Easy students never taught a teacher anything.

Control Outside the Classroom

Extra-classroom assignments vary tremendously from school to school. The modern trend, heaven be praised, is to relieve teachers of the more arduous duties on the eminently sensible theory that if you hire a person to teach, he'll do more of it and do it better if you see that he has the time and strength left to teach. Few schools today, for example, require the teacher to carry in wood and coal and keep the classroom stove going as our predecessors routinely did a century ago.

Typically, a teacher's assignments nowadays might include: selling tickets for and chaperoning sports events and dances; hall, cafeteria, restroom, and bus supervision; sponsorship of clubs; and membership on P.T.A. committees. In these instances the teacher bears no responsibility to teach anything, and in all assignments but the last, retains only the responsibility for handling discipline. In fact, that's the reason he's there.

CHAPERONING

Chaperoning sports events and dances can be fun rather than a chore. In most schools, problems rarely arise; you may attend these affairs for a couple of years and never hear an angry word. Besides that, seeing your students at play is a surprising and delightful experience. The wildest dance on the floor may be executed by the mousy little girl in your third-period class. And who turns out to be the best tackle on the second team? The Timeserver you've been worrying about for weeks!

When you attend school events, dress appropriately. Your principal expects you to—but more than that, your students expect you to. Although you won't be aware of it, many pairs of eyes will be taking your measure.

"There's my physics teacher over there. See her?"

"The witch in the horse blanket?"

"Naw, you jerk, not her. The gal in the blue suit."

"Oh. *Her.* Looks okay."

For sports affairs, the sort of thing you wear to school is good. This same type of clothing is appropriate for informal student dances. It is not appropriate, however, for a prom or other formal party. You will never be forgiven if you chaperone a formal dance or banquet in jeans. This will be a party that has been planned and looked forward to all year. The girls will have agonized for weeks deciding whether to buy the white satin pants suit or the blue brocade mini. The boys will have spent sweaty hours earning money for corsages and for a post-dance treat. Intricate arrangements will have been made concerning the music, the ballroom decorations, the Grand March, and the selection of the master of ceremonies. For a chaperone to treat all this as just one more throwaway evening is a cruel affront.

It is an equally bad mistake for women teachers to move too far in the opposite direction. Don't try to match the girls' party finery; try to make a fitting background for them. Something subdued. Men should definitely wear suits and ties.

Students will ask you to dance and if your're a good dancer, a brief venture on the dance floor will raise your status in the classroom. Then go sit down and stay there. Decline invitations with a smile and a plausible excuse. ("My wife doesn't like it if I dance too much with beautiful girls.") These affairs are for the students, not the faculty. There is something unseemly about a faculty member who pretends he's just a kid at heart. The price he pays in damaged prestige is too high for the fun he has.

At any large school function, the principal or vice principal will be on hand to give you the evening's instructions. Follow them. Once you've taken your "battle station," look around from time to time, although it may be hard to remember to do so if it's a good football game you're supervising. Investigate students who have gathered in a knot behind the bleachers to watch something. Find out what the something is they're watching. Break it up if it shouldn't be going on.

Be alert for loud arguments. They grow into fights and then into full-scale donneybrooks, and it can happen while you take the time to summon the vice principal. Don't wait that long. Get to it immediately while it's still at the argument stage. Collect ID cards from the students involved. Straighten it out on the spot, if you can. If not, take the students with you to find the vice principal.

Most schools keep one or more uniformed policemen on duty. It's nice to know where they are in case you need them.

Although women teachers are usually excused from the tougher assignments at these gatherings, one wonders if they should be. An angry woman strikes as much awe in students as an angry man, and sometimes more.

Watch out for drugs, booze, visitors, and weapons, in that order. Joints and intoxicants will most often be brought on the premises by girls, not boys. Girls have more places to hide them. Once inside, your nose will tell you which students are smoking grass and drinking.*

*Of course you will be able to detect the odor because you won't have been smoking grass or drinking yourself.

It's safe to say that the big high school dance is on the decline, partly because of drugs, and partly because of increased crime. Having a big dance at a school is like turning on a light: it attracts bugs from miles around. Toughs from other schools, and former students from your own school who have been expelled or who have dropped out, take this opportunity to stir up a little excitement. Since they aren't bona fide students, there is no way to control them once they are admitted. Usually, school policy forbids admitting them at all. They will hang around the building or the parking lot if they aren't chased away, which is why supervision is necessary over the entire area, not just the room where the dance is being held.

If only enrolled students are admitted, there will be no problem with weapons. The students will tend to abide by the same rules that govern them when classes are going on during the day, and penalties for carrying weapons are severe.

If drinks are dispensed via machine in bottles, the empty bottles should be returned to their cases promptly and not left at random over the premises to become handy weapons if a fight breaks out. A better plan is to have a refreshment stand as close to the dance area as possible to provide drinks in paper cups. You can't split anybody's head open with a paper cup. But as more school authorities are discovering, the paper-cup-route splits heads open from the inside. Soft drinks in paper cups can easily be spiked with LSD.

FIGHTS

Whether at a social or sports affair or during the school day, a big, planned fight is a bad scene. Bad for everybody. Advance warning of the battle usually manages to leak out several hours before it occurs. Boys tell their girlfriends. The girlfriends don't want the boyfriends to get hurt. The girlfriends squeal to the teachers in hopes the fight will be stopped before it starts. If a girlfriend squeals to you, stop the fight before it starts, but *don't squeal on her*. Get all the information you can. Who are the battle captains? Where and when is the confrontation scheduled to take place? How many are involved? Don't waste time. Get the information to the vice principal as soon as possible.

Sometimes these fights will be racial contests, in which case there may not be any real reason behind them at all. The blacks may simply be out to get the whites or the Chicanos may simply be out to get the blacks. There may be chains, knives, razors, and rocks for weapons.

The only thing to do if a full-scale fight breaks out is to get as much help as possible and then begin at the edge pulling kids out of it. Work in toward the middle. Keep yelling something that sounds official, like "Break it up! Break it up!" so they'll know you're a teacher. Look for the kids with the weapons and get them as soon as you can. The ones who started it will probably be the hardest of all to stop. Get them to the office or to a room away from the rest of the mob where everybody can cool off and talk sense. Get the vice principal or the cops and let them handle it. Go back out and help disperse the crowd.

So much for the planned battle. What about small-scale fights that erupt on the schoolground, at a football game, or at a dance? Boys' fights are never as spontaneous as they may appear to be on the surface. They represent an accumulation of less-than-fight-sized resentments that finally build up intolerable pressure. If the pressure is strong enough, a trivial remark can trigger a fight. Typically, one boy will bully and taunt another over a long period of time. At length, the bully pushes his luck too far and the underdog fights back.

When two boys fight each other they pound and break a few bones, if possible. Girls' fights are bloodier and messier. They claw, tear, gouge, and rip. A whole army of boys might join and fight side by side with the original combatants but there will never be more than two girls. Boys get into fights on their own, but for girls there's always a "promoter."

"Julia said you were two-faced."

"*Me* two-faced! What about *her?* She's the one who's two-faced!"

"Kathy said you were the most two-faced b- - - - in school."

"You tell Kathy for me that her mother should have flushed her down the john before she was a week old."

"Julia said she'd like to flush you down the john."

"She did, did she? I'd like to see her try it, that dirty, no-good #%@ #&%!"

"Kathy's going to beat you up."

"Just tell me when and where and we'll see about that."

"This afternoon after school. There's a good place in the alley behind the grocery store."

The promoter will hustle up a crowd and may or may not stop short of selling tickets. The vice principal will be looking for the promoter, and so should you if it falls your job to round everybody up.

A final note about fights. When an ugly situation threatens, it will be a temptation for the new teacher to disappear behind a closed door until the dust settles, leaving the principal and vice principal to straighten it out as best they can. That's his privilege, but before he turns tail and runs, he should try to imagine how the principal will feel about the desertion. He won't say anything, but he'll think plenty. Once the new teacher has handed the principal a lousy deal like that, he shouldn't make the mistake of asking the principal for any favors. It will be a waste of breath.

SELLING TICKETS

Selling tickets at the game or dance is pretty tame for the teacher. The worst hazards are frostbite if the ticket booth is drafty, and that limp feeling when you realize you gave a customer ten dollars' worth of change for his five. Things are slow after the game starts. Bring a magazine. There will be security measures about the money. Observe them to the letter.

"I CAN'T MAKE IT"

Suppose you have been assigned duty at an evening activity and a wheel drops off your car and you simply can't make it. Be sure to let someone in authority know, just as you would if you couldn't take your classes during the day. If your chaperoning assignment falls on the night you planned to go bowling, offer to exchange assignments with another teacher. Or pay another teacher to take it. It isn't unheard of for enterprising young teachers to do a flourishing business taking unwanted duty assignments for a fee.

HALL, CAFETERIA, AND BUS DUTY

Hall duty simply means walking a beat. It's a good time for making grocery lists or organizing next week's lesson plans. You may be asked to patrol the hall immediately outside your classroom door while students are passing from one class to another. Whether this is required or not, it's good psychology to greet your students at the door. The gesture evokes the same overtones as a host with his guests. "You are expected and welcome," it says, and your students will sit up a bit straighter because you gave them that feeling.

Like hall duty, nothing much is likely to happen when your turn comes to supervise the cafeteria during lunch period. You may need to remind a few negligent youngsters to do whatever it is they're supposed to do with their trays. If a student makes a mess, make him clean it up. There's not one chance in fifty that an argument will start—but if it does, break it up *immediately*. A cafeteria is the yuckiest place imaginable for a fight.

When you're on bus duty, all you do is watch the busses drive up, load, and drive off. Holler around a little if the students seem inclined to shove.

RESTROOM DUTY

Women teachers have a rougher time of it than men when it comes to restroom duty. Girls throw used paper towels on the floor, foul the basins with hair combings, and write filthy poems on the walls.

If you catch a student contributing to the pig-sty effect, make her clean it up, of course. Report the filthy poem to the vice principal, who will have the custodian remove it as soon as possible before it inspires still another Emily Dickinson to add a couplet or two.

Your school will probably be careful about cleaning away all graffiti daily. This is partly because one good mark suggests another. But it is also because if you know the restroom was clean at the beginning of the day, it's easier to find the culprit if it is *not* clean at, say, 9 A.M. You narrow the field down to the people who were there during an hour and a half, instead of suspecting the people who were there over a two-day period.

Smoking is the big problem in the restrooms, and the unfairness of the situation gives school people a slow burn. In one California county, there hasn't been an arrest for selling tobacco to minors in 25 years—yet the pressure remains as heavy as ever on school officials to enforce no-smoking rules. Both state laws and school policy will forbid student smoking on the school premises. (This is tobacco we're talking about, remember. For pot, see below.) All you can do is punish the glaring offenses and nit-pick away at the others in a battle that no one will ever win.

When you enter a restroom and witness two or three students actually holding cigarettes, collar them immediately and take them to the office. If you are assigned total supervisory responsibility for one restroom—say, across the hall from your classroom—don't be so regular about your policing that the smokers can set their watches by you. One day check at 9:15, 1:30, and 3. Next day, check at 8:30, 9:00, and 2. Report all incidents of smoking and vandalism to the vice principal.

POT

Experts estimate that more than six million U.S. young people of high school and college age have tried marijuana at least once. Some are going to try it in your school. Whether or not the use of marijuana ever becomes legalized, the drug has no place in the schools. The smell of marijuana smoke is as easy to identify as the smell of booze. You might catch a whiff of it while chaperoning a ball game, checking the restrooms, or standing close to a student in your class. If you haven't been given instructions for handling such occurrences, jot down the details, sign the note, and leave it in the vice principal's box at the end of the day.

CLUB SPONSORSHIP

Running a student activity can be a business in itself. The yearbook organization may maintain an office, hire clerical help, and collect and disburse thousands of dollars a year. Sponsoring clubs and activities is nearly always done on a volunteer basis; the more experienced teachers are favored for the bigger assignments, which sometimes yield a modest stipend. This is a blessing in disguise for the first-year teacher, who will have more corn than he can hoe, anyway.

Once he has his classes under control, the new teacher might find it valuable to ally himself with an older, experienced teacher-sponsor in the role of assistant—a painless way to learn the student-activity ropes. He may, of course, be assigned a small club the first year. This is not such a painless way to learn the ropes. But if he finds out what to do about the money and does it, and obtains extra supervisory help with parties, cookouts, and the like, he should get along all right. He would do well to remember that in a club, you let down—but only about halfway.

Sponsoring a student organization means that sooner or later you must ask other teachers to excuse your members from class to do something about the club. Protocol must be observed in such matters. First of all, get your principal's permission for the project. Then about ten days before the trip, type up a ditto master that runs something like this:

Dear _____,

On Thursday, October 26, from 1 P.M. to 4 P.M., the Chess Club members would like to attend the state chess tournament being held in our city. Club members understand that they may go only with the permission of their teachers and with the understanding they are to make up work missed in classes that day.

Our club roster is as follows:

(List of members)

If you are willing to excuse these students from your classes that afternoon, will you please initial this letter and return it to the student presenting it?

Cordially yours,
(Your name)
Chess Club Sponsor

Fill in the appropriate teacher's name at the top and assign a student to deliver the forms one day and pick them up the next. If there seems to be an objection anywhere, go around to see the teacher personally and answer any question he has. You will nearly always be able to work out any difficulties together. Be sure to thank the teacher for his co-operation.

The new teacher, in his turn, will be on the receiving end of requests from other club sponsors. He should co-operate, if possible, but he isn't expected to co-operate to the point of completely rejuggling his lesson plans. If many students are involved and it means a real inconvenience for him, he should go to the sponsor as soon as possible and see what can be worked out. Maybe the sponsor can change his date.

THE P.T.A.

The P.T.A. is a strong national organization. It has clout in Washington that has been used on more than one occasion to tip the legislative scales in favor of the nation's schools. The chances are that your principal will support your local organization.

One day he will call you into his office and ask you if you will serve on the P.T.A. refreshment or program committee. Since he heads up the "T" part of the P.T.A., he must furnish personnel to help make the thing go.

Don't be surprised if you discover your committee work is more enjoyable than the monthly meetings you will be helping to put on. Parents can be fun. Some P.T.A. groups have better luck with one yearly blast—a parent's night, a "fair" or "carnival" to raise money—something like that. Others go the once-a-month meeting route. A handful of souls will clip-clop their way through the school's deserted evening corridors to hear a lady report there is $26.15 in the treasury, after which a panel of adolescents will explain how the school's student government works. Coffee or punch will be served in the home economics room, and everybody will say what a shame there wasn't a better turnout to hear the nice program.

Some principals, as a pump-priming device, let it be known that teachers are expected to be at the P.T.A. meetings. This is a good way to get out a crowd of teachers, but it makes for soggy morale in the long run. It puts the outnumbered parents on the defensive, and soon you've got a monthly teachers' meeting.

The chances of seeing the parents of your students at the average P.T.A. meeting are miniscule. However, there will be a full-dress evening affair sometime in the fall, which may be sponsored by the P.T.A. or some other group. The classrooms will be open, with teachers inside and available for parent-teacher conferences. These are often well attended—never by the parents you need most to see, of course—but you may put in a busy evening chatting with mamas and papas. Be a good host. Meet as many people at the door as you can. Invite them in and ask them to sit down. You will have written your name on the chalkboard, but introduce yourself anyway. "How do you do? I'm Mr. Lansdale. It's good of you to come."

Most parents will introduce themselves as "Ted Smith's parents." After a few pleasantries, they will ask if Ted is doing all right, whereupon you will consult your gradebook, if necessary, and reassure them that he is. Kids with parents interested enough to come to meet their teachers usually are.

Rarely, you will have parents whose children are in difficulties. When that happens, get the student's papers, your gradebook, or whatever you need from your desk and sit down with these people somewhere else in the room besides your desk. If you seat yourself behind your desk, it implies that somehow the parents are students, too, and you are demanding things of them. You want to establish rapport, but you won't do it that way.

Of all the allies you can enlist in helping you to handle a student in your classroom, none will be more valuable than that student's parents. Parents can see that the homework gets done, that the student gets to school on time, and that he gets enough sleep so he doesn't doze off in class. Most important of all for the purposes of this book, ties of friendship and support at home can virtually eliminate that student's misbehavior in your classroom. Extra effort spent talking to parents is bread cast upon the waters that comes back petit fours. Every time.

Show the parents first of all that you respect their child as a fellow human being. Show them you know his strengths and weaknesses and know what to do about them—in short, show them that you know your business. Enlist their support as partners in a joint enterprise, helping their son or daughter to achieve as much as possible in school.

It's a good idea to rub elbows with people in the community where you teach. Whether you live there or not, you can trade there, get to know the gas station people, the supermarket manager, the barber, the druggist. Let them know you are a booster, that their tax dollars are staying in the community.

In Loco Parentis

Once upon a time the school's authority was well defined. Teachers and principals served *in loco parentis*—"in place of the parent." In recent years the concept has undergone legal erosion; still, in practice at least, our roles resemble those of parents so closely that the psychodynamics of child-parent relationships at home find their counterpart in pupil-teacher relationships at school. We should pay more attention to those forces. We'd learn a lot.

An old pro with twenty-five years of teaching experience once said, "If both the mother and the father are strict, the kid gets along okay. If both the mother and the father are lenient, the kid gets along okay. But when one parent is strict and the other parent is lenient, you've got a kid with more hang-ups than an argyle sock. Watch out!"

She was right, too. I've seen the proof in my pupils as you will see the proof in yours. Children raised in the kind of ambivalent environment described by my friend learn destructive lessons. They learn that

1. There is no such thing as right and wrong.

2. Rules and promises were made to be broken. "Yes" never means yes. "No" never means no. Both are subject to veto.

3. In this world nothing is certain—nothing. Not for anybody, anywhere, anytime.

4. People in authority are to be hated and feared. Who knows what they'll do?

If such lessons are learned in ambivalent homes, what about our ambivalent schools? On one hand we have the lenient counselor who serves as advocate for the problem student in the school. That's what the counselor's job *is*, mind you. That's what he's been hired to do. The counselor must understand the problem

student, overlook his faults, and forgive his transgressions in an attempt to help the youngster solve his own problems.

On the other hand we have the stern assistant principal. What has he been hired to do? His job is to enforce the school's rules and punish offenders—i.e., the problem student. His task is to ferret out and chastise the very transgressions the counselor wants to forgive and forget. These adults, who represent the senior officials of the school, are working at cross purposes, each undermining the authority of the other. So where are we today?

Student respect for school authority has sunk to such a low point in some districts that the proper business of the school—education—can scarcely be carried on at all.

The problem of the counselor versus the assistant principal makes a convenient object lesson because of its high visibility. Other insidious examples of undermined authority exist everywhere in the school, as we will see in the following examples.

EXAMPLE A: The police have notified the school authorities that a drug pusher has been operating out of the sandwich shop across the street. The sandwich shop has been declared off limits for students, but a teacher who thinks of herself as The Student's Pal resents the principal's edict. She says she'll eat lunch at the sandwich shop if she pleases. And she does. "The kids know I won't fink on them, don't you, kids? That story about their selling dope over here is silly."

The students think: "If the principal is such a jerk he can't get his own teachers to do what he says, why should I do what he says?" Or, "That teacher is just as liable to get into trouble as I am. When she does, will she think one of us kids squealed on her? What will she do then? Is she really what she pretends to be, the student's pal, or is she some kind of spy? Whose side is she on, anyway?"

EXAMPLE B: The angry teacher says, "What d'you mean, the assistant principal won't let you smoke on the schoolgrounds? Next time that %¢&*&¢% gives you a bunch of his crap, tell him to shove it. You don't have to take nothing off that S.O.B."

The students think: "Suppose I do what the teacher says and get detention or get kicked out. The teacher won't get in trouble, I will. Where will the teacher be if that happens?" Or, "Listen to the Big Man talk! Next time he chews me out because I didn't get my work in on time, maybe I won't take any crap off *him*, either!"

Multiply examples like these by a dozen or so every day, sprinkled over the school from the P.E. department to the nurse's office, and you'll have an institution peopled with insolent, rebellious teen-age cynics as sure as God made little green apples.

Presenting a united front to students simply isn't all that hard to do. It doesn't mean that all teachers in the school must agree. They won't, so forget that. What the teachers *can* do is settle their disagreements privately. They can show students that they respect one another. They can refuse to vie for student loyalties like dogs snarling over a bone.

The new teacher should be ready for the tale-bearing student. Take him with a grain of salt. There may be some truth to the story he tells you about the chalk-throwing incident in Mr. A's room, but there may also be some truth that's left out of what he tells you. If for some reason you need to get the straight story of the incident, ask for Mr. A's version. The best policy is to discourage this kind of gossiping altogether, either with students or with teachers.

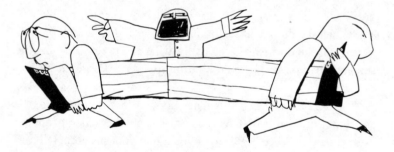

Occasionally, two teachers will find themselves competing for a student's time. Perhaps you have told a student he must stay after school and bring his lab notebook up to date. He says he can't because Mr. B told him to stay after school for *him* to do his math assignment. Don't waste everyone's time sending this student back and forth with messages. Go see the teacher yourself with the student in tow. Make your arrangements with Mr. B so that everyone understands what the student is to do and when.

Making derogatory statements to your classes about assemblies, the athletic program, the school in general, is a pernicious sort of nitpicking. What's worse, it boomerangs. To announce "This class did 20 percent better than Mr. C's class on the biology test" delivers a gratuitous slap at Mr. C and diminishes his prestige with his students, each and every one of whom, you may be quite sure, will hear the jolly news. It is better to say, "This class did remarkably well on the biology test," which serves the same purpose without malice.

If crystal balls could be checked from the A-V department, you would discover that twenty-five years from now there will be some members of your school's college-prep classes who will have ended up on Skid Row and some members of the slow-learner classes who will be making five-figure salaries. Ability-grouped classes should be taken seriously as a teaching convenience, that's all. As prognosticators of future student success, they are pretty poor. As indicators of the intrinsic worth of either students or teachers assigned to them, they are hopeless.

Before you make snide remarks to your students about the remedial classes, bear in mind that some of the college-prep history students you're talking to may be enrolled in remedial mathematics courses.

Avoid putting on airs if you are assigned an honors class. You might look silly. Some districts start all beginners there because a novice teacher can do less damage to the gifted than to any other group. The gifted will learn in spite of the new teacher's mistakes.

"We're late to class because Mr. D made us do twenty-five push-ups for being noisy."

Privately, you may react to this information in a number of

different ways, one of which might be to resolve to see Mr. D before the day is over to find out what really happened. Regardless of your feeling about it, however, you would be well-advised to comment, "Probably did you good. Now take your seats and let's get started or I may have you do twenty-five more."

"My counselor wouldn't even answer my question. He just walked off and left me standing there. A counselor's not supposed to act like that. Can't I report him?"

"Maybe he walked off because he was going someplace to report you."

"My math teacher is an old crab. He doesn't even try to understand his students. Can I transfer to your class?"

"I've got news for you. I'm just as crabby as the math teacher you've got now, and I don't understand you either. You're better off where you are."

The new teacher should make every attempt to get to know the counselors, particularly those of his more troublesome students. The counselor seldom hears anything but the student's version—the *aggrieved* student's version—of what goes on in the classroom. Since the counselor is seldom in the classroom himself, he tends to forget his own years of teaching and the realities of hour-to-hour, day-to-day teaching. He comes to expect teachers, who must handle the student as one in a group of thirty, and the administrator, who must handle him as one in fifteen hundred, to exercise the same understanding tolerance he himself is able to command when talking to the student alone in the privacy of his office. With a steady diet of student confidences and virtually no teacher confidences at all, he comes to see all his students a good bit purer than they are, and both teachers and administrators as a good bit more villanous than they really are.

The counselor's role, under the best of circumstances, is not a happy one. He rests squarely on the horns of the individual-versus-society dilemma, which hasn't been resolved in the last ten thousand years and isn't likely to be resolved before he retires.

LOOKING AHEAD

Yes, your first year will be rough. There'll be discipline problems aplenty and there may be times when you'll want to quit. Don't. Each grueling week you win will mean a week of satisfying teaching next year—and the year after that.

Satisfying, yes, but it will be hard work. The enormous physical demands, plus the emotional pressure, plus the noise—all these elements take their toll. Outsiders are wont to complain that teachers are politically and socially indifferent. They aren't indifferent; they're tired!

The new teacher will begin to realize what he's gotten himself into around Thanksgiving of his first year. His training will have prepared him to cope with his responsibilities. But whether or not his morale and his physical stamina will support maximum use of that training is another question.

What does all this have to do with control? Everything. When a teacher begins to tire, to suffer from months and years of accumulated fatigue, the first place it shows is in his discipline. He has more trouble finding time for conferences with the counselor about problem students. He becomes negligent about following up on petty offenses. He takes refuge in haranguing students

rather than actually coming to grips with problems in constructive ways. His classes tend to get out of hand and he thinks,
"They're a little loud today." As the months pass, and his students
become successively "a little louder," he is able to teach them "a
little less." One deterioration feeds the other.

The more progressive schools, in their concern to protect
teaching efficiency over ten- to forty-year periods, make administrative provision for avoiding "teacher erosion." It is not uncom-
mon nowadays to hear of schools that grant sabbaticals, that
actively encourage "teacher exchanges," that grant leaves of absence for teachers to work at jobs away from the district, or that
maintain a policy of moving teachers from assignment to assignment within the school district.

Whether he becomes conscious of the problem at the end of
two months, two years, or twenty years of teaching, however,
there is much the teacher himself can do to avoid battle fatigue.
(That's all it is, really.)

He needs a hobby, for one thing. Listening to phonograph
records or (if the teacher is a woman) hooking rugs won't do. The
mind is still free to brood about school problems. The activity
must be absorbing, must call for physical and mental activity, not
passivity. Bowling, gourmet cooking with a congenial group,
reading, carpentry, painting, and choral singing are all good.

Keep in training. Get enough sleep, eat a balanced diet and get
the proper exercise. The demands of teaching are rigorous even
for a person in good health. A sick person will crumple out of
shape in no time at all.

Try to arrange matters so you don't have to take courses at
night while school is going on, ever. This is especially true during
your first year. This is entirely too big a dose of new educational
experiences to absorb at one time. You won't learn much, either
from your professor or from your new students.

You will probably need to pick up courses in summer school

(doesn't everybody?). Try to schedule the ones you need so you won't go all summer and return to school in the fall as exhausted as when you left in June. Make the time count that you spend on the college campus with real honest-to-goodness adults. You'll pick up as many new ideas from the other students in your classes as you will from the professor. Have coffee with them; study with them. The best ploy of all is to find a principal in the class who's fifty miles or more from home. (Not a local product; he'll be afraid you might quote him.) Buy him a couple of beers and get him to talk shop. You'll *really* learn about education!

Take a course in something unrelated to your field but that you've always wanted to know more about—music appreciation, ceramics, Egyptology, investments, Elizabethan poets, scuba diving, or archaeology.

Get away from home. Load up the family and take a boat trip down a river, camp out in the mountains, rent a cabin on the lake, visit your brother in Florida, teach summer school in another city (*not* your own district!).

Allow yourself a week to get ready for school in the fall when you go back. Go through your files; throw away things you know you won't use again. Develop teaching ideas and new lesson plans; revise your old tests; work out that new bulletin board display. Write companies for catalogs or examination copies of books; write to that expert in your field or a former professor for a point of information you aren't sure about. Set up your calendar for the year. Approximately when will you need to order this? When will you check out that? When will you invite the guest speakers?

Do you like your room arrangement the way it is? Is your desk farther from the door than you'd like it to be? Do the students get afternoon sun in their eyes? Are you tired of the pictures? Change things around.

Most important, try to see it all as a whole. "What am I doing and why?" Teaching isn't like running a grocery store or filling teeth or selling insurance. Maybe it's more like farming than anything else. Every year there's a new crop. "Success" means the crop grew and flourished and "failure" means it didn't. The growing season demands grueling, backbreaking work. Teachers and farmers don't rest much over weekends, as others do, but once a year, during the off-season.

There are good years and bad years. There are years when the seed is right, the soil perfect, the rains on time, and the farmer can do no wrong. Other years everything he does goes wrong. Both farmers and teachers learn to accept these cycles, even to exploit them.

One perseveres. Last year's mistakes inspire this year's experiments, which in turn yield next year's wisdom. So, one grows with the growing, finds renewal in the renewed. Perhaps that's why teachers and farmers live longer than other people do. It's a good life, after all.

Index